THE TRUTH ABOUT MENTAL TOUGHNESS IN SPORTS

INTERVIEWS STRAIGHT FROM THE PROS

PROVEN STRATEGIES TO BUILD CONFIDENCE,
TURN SETBACKS INTO FOCUS, AND ACHIEVE
PEAK PERFORMANCE FOR YOUNG ATHLETES

TONY NEUMEYER

CONTENTS

"Mental toughness is believing without a doubt that you will come out on top. It's focusing on the process, not the result."

TIM GROVER (TRAINER OF MICHAEL JORDAN AND KOBE BRYANT)

INTRODUCTION

 "You have to be able to accept failure to get better. There's no shortcut. You have to trust the process and stick with it."

LEBRON JAMES

You could say that it ran in her blood.

Emma Vlasic started skating at age two and playing boys' hockey at five. Her brothers also played, so hockey was a big part of the family's life. She played boys' hockey until age thirteen, which included a full year of body checking.

Emma's earliest memories of hockey are on the backyard rink her dad built every winter in their Wilmette, Illinois home. It wasn't much—a few boards, some frozen water—but to young Emma, it was an arena. She spent hours skating, shooting, and imagining herself scoring the winning goal in a championship game. "It was always me against my brothers," she laughed. "Sometimes I won. Sometimes I didn't. But I always wanted to play again."

Her dedication to the sport required sacrifice, diligence, and dedication. It wasn't always easy or fun. But as is the case with many youth sports, each lump she took had taught her a lesson.

All her time playing hockey with the boys readied her to move to the Tier One girls' team with her age group, known as level U14 in the international hockey world.

She went on and played Tier One until U19 and then moved on to play in college at Yale. However, things got tougher that first year. Given her top level of play, she expected to contribute and play immediately, but that's not what happened.

In her words, "You think you're good, and then you go into college, and you realize, okay, this is a whole other level. My first year was tough. I didn't play a lot. I didn't really get the most out of what I thought I was capable of."

In our interview, she talks about an eight-hour bus trip from New Haven to Saint Lawrence. It's a trip she won't forget, as she later knew that the journey had helped to inspire her. "I dressed but didn't step foot on the ice once. So yeah, it's mentally tough," she said.

After pausing for a moment, she continued, "80% of the game is mental, especially when you reach these levels." At about the midpoint in her sophomore year, she started to turn things around. She began to understand the mental aspects of the game. Mentally changing some of her approaches, she increased her confidence, grounded herself, and allowed herself the confidence to grow further.

"Confidence is such a big part of it, and I didn't have that confidence during the first year and a half of playing. It was my junior year when that really took off for me."

Emma had put in all her time at the gym as required to play at this level, and her stick and skating skills were grounded there too. What she did was simple but crucial to her play on the ice; she adopted a two-word mantra that worked.

"I wanted to be calm and confident going into the game and to know that I belonged out there and could contribute at the highest level." Before each game, she'd take a few minutes to gather herself and repeat these words: "'Calm and confident.' Those were my two words going into a game."

Emma became captain of the Yale Hockey Team and went on to play for the Connecticut Whale, a women's professional hockey team, where she was among the best players and became alternate captain.

Late one day after a particularly tough game, Emma found herself in the locker room with her dejected team, the weight of responsibility heavy on her shoulders. Looking around, she knew that a fiery speech wouldn't fit what they all needed. Instead, she quietly pulled aside a struggling teammate and offered words of encouragement. "It wasn't about yelling," she explained afterward. "It was about making sure everyone knew we were in this together." That calm leadership became her trademark, both on and off the ice.

To say that grasping the mental part of the game is what took her to new heights is not an overstatement. Emma's career and story are very personal to her. Still, when you look at the bigger picture across all sports, what Emma had concluded is not unusual.

Have you ever wondered why some people with exceptional talent make it to their respective sports' elite or higher professional levels, while others with similar talent just never reach those same goals?

In the many I've been involved with sports professionals, some of whom I've known as good friends, such realizations about achievement has been a topic of discussion at times.

What you'll discover in this book is how you can have your best shot at making it to those elite levels. What I'm about to show you is that the difference, in many cases, is about your razor's edge. You'll come to understand that very fine difference, and it's one with which you can reach success.

I'll detail what I mean by razor's edge shortly, so you can understand it fully and implement it in your life and training sessions.

The title of this book, The Truth About Mental Toughness, gives you a clue, but it doesn't tell the whole story. Part of the truth is that *you are in charge of you,* and another aspect is that *there are no excuses.* Don't get me wrong; I can't guarantee that by reading this book or even implementing everything in it, you'll make it to the big leagues. However, I can guarantee that if you follow the practices in this book and the videos, you'll be a better, stronger person, and the habits you create will carry you far, wherever your journey leads you.

The first two quotes earlier in this book to point you in a direction that I will soon detail, unravel, and help you create your personal process. By the end of this book, you will know and can develop the path that's right for you.

Your coaches may already have a system for you to follow, and I hope they do. However, you, too, can have an additional process that makes you stronger, more resilient, and simply better every day. As I said, no matter what you accomplish in life, your ability to create your own process for success and mental toughness will carry you well through your entire life.

When I said there are 'no excuses,' I was talking about creating and following a step-by-step plan, personalized for your achievement at the highest levels. Results will come when you stick with routines that build mental and physical strength over time. What's amazing is that your small incremental changes done consistently will result in major changes down the road, and often much sooner than you think. As we talk about the goals, how to use them, and how they can be manifested in your life, your key to success is in understanding that small changes over time make huge gains.

Success comes with knowing what to do and doing it. On the other hand, I've seen numerous young athletes struggle with self-doubt and setbacks. Some did well in sports; others left professional sports and went on to greatness in other areas. I want to arm you with strategies that are not just theories but proven methods that work.

I know you face challenges in balancing school, training, and your personal life. This book is also for parents who want to support their aspiring athletes and for coaches needing ways to inspire their athletes. Developing mental toughness is not an easy journey, but it is essential. Together, we will explore and tackle these challenges.

Mental toughness is the backbone of success, both on and off the field. Studies show that athletes with high mental resilience perform better and handle stress more effectively. But it's not just about winning games; it's about building character and preparing for life's many challenges. Mental toughness is critical, whether dealing with a formidable opponent or bouncing back from a disappointing loss.

You will discover that mental and physical toughness are often intertwined. By the end of this book, you will have the tools to face challenges head-on and emerge stronger. I will share actionable strategies for you to build your confidence and resilience. We'll draw from the experiences of professional athletes who've been where you are now and have come out on top.

As mentioned, I've interviewed professional athletes for this book for you to reference and learn from. At the end of the book, I will have a link for you to view each interview in full, and I give a short biography of each professional. Additionally, throughout the book, I have shared quotes from their interviews to help give you insights into what it took for them to make it to professional leagues.

Three of the athletes whom I've quoted in this guide are from team sports, while one comes from an individual sport. Each has different perspectives on how they approach their sport. Still, one thing is obvious: Mental toughness played a significant role in their success.

In this book, you'll find a roadmap to building your mental strength. You won't just learn what to do; you'll see how others have done it. From professionals, Olympians, and world champions, their journeys will inspire and guide you. The insights in the interviews and seeing them all laid out in this book bring us strategies to life, making these real insights easier to understand and implement.

Before we dive deeper, let me introduce some of the athletes whose insights have shaped this book. Below, I've shared a comparative short bio for each person, so you can get a real feel for who is offering their encouragement and advice. Their experiences will help illustrate what it takes to develop mental toughness and succeed at the highest levels.

Michael Saunders is a former Major League Baseball player. Drafted by the Seattle Mariners, he played eight seasons in the

MLB and transitioned into coaching and player development after his retirement. His story is one of perseverance, adapting to new environments, and building confidence in the face of challenges.

Emma Vlasic, who you've just met, is a professional women's hockey player who played for the Yale Bulldogs and the Connecticut Whale. Her journey highlights the importance of confidence, resilience, and mental preparation. Mastering athletic achievement has brought her knowledge about how to work in a larger playing field, and she is currently with Hedgeye, an independent market research firm.

Eric Wood, an eight-year professional baseball player, offers insights into consistency, routines, and the mindset required to stay competitive. He is currently the Director of Player Development with Prospects Park in Englewood, CO.

Jasper Blake, a world-renowned triathlon champion, brings a unique perspective as an individual sport athlete. He emphasizes the incremental changes and consistent efforts that lead to extraordinary results. He now currently heads up B78 Coaching in BC, Canada.

Now, let's focus on you. I invite you to take this journey with me. We'll work with each other to build your personal methods into the mental toughness you need to achieve peak performance. Use the tools and insights in this book to transform your approach to sports and life. The path to becoming a mentally tough athlete starts here. Let's get started.

CHAPTER 1
BUILDING YOUR BACKBONE: THE CORE OF MENTAL TOUGHNESS

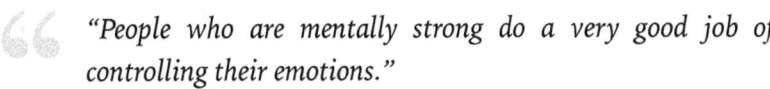

"People who are mentally strong do a very good job of controlling their emotions."

ERIC WOOD

A young basketball player once faced a seemingly insurmountable challenge. Her team was down by ten points with just two minutes left on the clock.

The pressure was intense and could make anyone's knees buckle.

But instead of crumbling, she rallied her team, focusing not on the scoreboard but on each play. They turned the game around with grit and determination, winning in overtime. This isn't just a tale of physical prowess but a testament to mental toughness.

But what exactly is mental toughness, and how do you build it? I'll answer this question as we lay out the groundwork for understanding this crucial component of athletic success.

UNDERSTANDING MENTAL TOUGHNESS

At its core, mental toughness is about resilience and strength. Mental endurance allows us to push through challenging situations, sometimes even physical pain, and stay on course when things get tough. Imagine facing a formidable opponent or dealing with a real setback, such as a serious injury.

Mental toughness is what keeps you going and helps you regulate your emotions under pressure. It helps you maintain consistent performance despite the odds. And it's more than just a single trait; it's a multifaceted skill set that combines emotional regulation, focus, and perseverance.

For you, developing mental toughness isn't just beneficial; it's essential. It equips you to handle the stress of competition with grace, enhances your concentration during pivotal moments, and builds a foundation for success in all areas of life.

Mental toughness also prepares you for life's challenges. In sports, you're constantly faced with situations that test your resilience, like missing a crucial shot or losing a game. The ability to bounce back from these setbacks, learn from them, and continue striving toward your goals is a hallmark of mental toughness.

These concepts had Michael Saunders looking inward at his personal life experiences. We know about this when he shared the following powerful insight: "When I started my MLB career, I'd let one bad game follow me to the next. But after watching my mom fight cancer, I realized, if she could face that with such grace, I could survive a 0-for-4 day. That shift in perspective allowed me to play with freedom, and it made all the difference."

Michael used to joke that baseball came second to salmon fishing. Growing up on Vancouver Island, summers weren't just about getting ready for and playing in baseball tournaments—they were for early mornings on the water with his dad, reeling in Chinook salmon.

It wasn't lost on him how the two activities were similar: the patience required, the anticipation, and the explosive moment when preparation met opportunity. "In both, you learn quickly that you won't succeed every time," he said. "But the effort is always worth it."

Michael often found himself practicing in the rain. There were no pristine fields or year-round training facilities. "We'd shovel puddles off the diamond," he recalled. But it was in those soggy conditions that he developed a certain grit—a willingness to persevere when others might not even try.

Years later, in the sweltering heat of a Florida minor-league game, he thought back to those drizzly afternoons. The contrast made him smile. "If I could love the game in that weather," he mused, "I could love it anywhere."

Florida, with its sun-drenched fields and relentless competition, had given him an entirely different experience. "It was a culture shock," he admitted. "These guys had been playing year-round since they were kids. I had to prove to myself that I could keep up." But instead of letting the gap overwhelm him, Michael saw the challenge as an opportunity—a chance to grow. By the time the season ended, he knew he belonged.

Michael's first year of professional baseball was more humbling than triumphant. He had been a multi-sport standout in Canada, but when he joined teammates who had been playing year-round since they were kids, he realized just how far behind he was. At first, he struggled to adjust. But rather than let the whole situation defeat him; he became a student of the game. He analyzed swings, asked veterans for tips, and treated every mistake as a lesson. "By the end of the season," he said, "I wasn't the same player who showed up on day one."

Michael's journey to the Major Leagues wasn't without its share of mental hurdles. He recalls vividly the moment it all hit him—his first game against the Yankees, standing on the same field as players like Derek Jeter and Alex Rodriguez.

"I started playing against the names on the back of the jerseys, not the game itself," he said. It was a humbling realization, one that sent his performance spiraling downward. It wasn't until years later, after the passing of his mother, that he found clarity. "Seeing what my mom went through, I realized that a 0-for-4 day was only that one day in a larger time frame. I gave myself permission to fail, and that's when the game slowed down for me."

Mental toughness fosters an enhanced resilience that allows you to handle competition stress without breaking down. Improved focus and concentration on the field translate to better academic performance and more fulfilling interpersonal relationships off the field. When you build mental toughness, you're not just becoming a better athlete; you're becoming a more capable and resilient person.

In 2004, the Boston Red Sox were down three games to zero in the American League Championship Series against the New York Yankees. Their level of team toughness shone brightly in their remarkable comeback as they won four straight games, and the series, four games to three. Rest assured, each team member had mental toughness, contributing to the team's overall toughness.

They had finally ended the decades-long "Curse of the Bambino" that seemed destined to deny the Sox from ever winning baseball's greatest prize. Watching this series inspired Eric Wood to take up baseball and become a professional. He covers that in the video. If you don't have the mental toughness personally, you can't contribute to the toughness of your team.

Several core components form the backbone of mental toughness. Self-belief and confidence are the first pillars. As I wrote, Emma Vlasic discovered that she needed to get back her confidence when she began playing college hockey at Yale. She achieved this objective, which took her to the professional level of the game. Such core features empower you to trust in your abilities, even when others doubt you. This self-assurance fuels motivation and commitment, driving you to put in the extra hours of practice needed to excel.

Resilience and perseverance are the next layers. They allow you to keep pushing forward, even when faced with difficulties or failures. These elements work together to create a solid mental framework that supports your athletic and personal development. Each component interconnects, reinforcing the others to create a robust mental fortitude to withstand any challenge.

To illustrate how mental toughness plays out in real-world scenarios, consider the story of Roger Federer. Early in his career, Federer lost in the first round of Wimbledon for three consecutive years. Many athletes would have given up, but Federer used each loss as a learning experience. He analyzed his performance, identified areas for improvement, and worked tirelessly to improve his skills.

His perseverance paid off, and he won seven Wimbledon titles, solidifying his legacy as one of the greatest tennis players ever. Federer's story exemplifies how mental toughness helps athletes maintain composure in high-stakes situations and overcome adversity.

Another powerful example is the story of Jim Abbott, a one-handed pitcher who threw a no-hitter in Major League Baseball. Despite his physical challenges, Abbott's mental toughness allowed him to defy expectations. He developed an incredible focus and unwavering determination, proving that mental strength can overcome physical limitations.

These stories highlight that mental toughness isn't just about being strong in the moment; it's about building a mindset that prepares you for the long haul. It's about cultivating the grit and resilience required to face whatever challenges come your way, on and off the field.

THE SCIENCE BEHIND RESILIENCE

Resilience is like a superpower that helps athletes bounce back from setbacks and keep pushing forward.

Michael Saunders says, "Winning is about getting punched in the teeth, and you keep moving forward. Everyone can get hit physically, but not everyone can get hit mentally and continue to move forward."

What I'm sharing with you is not just about willpower; there's science behind it. Let's explore some psychological theories that explain how resilience develops in athletes. Psychologist Carol Dweck popularized the growth mindset theory. This mental state involves the belief that abilities and intelligence can be developed through dedication and hard work.

Such a mindset encourages athletes to embrace challenges, learn from mistakes, and see effort as a path to mastery. In contrast, a fixed mindset views abilities as static and unchangeable, leading to a fear of failure and avoidance of challenges. Developing a growth mindset can enhance resilience by fostering a love for learning and a willingness to persevere through difficulties.

Another psychological concept that plays a role in resilience is neuroplasticity; that is, the brain's ability to reorganize itself by forming new connections. This adaptability allows athletes to learn new skills, adapt to new situations, and recover from setbacks more effectively. The brain's capacity to change and grow means that resilience can be developed over time through intentional practice and mental conditioning.

One of the challenges for athletes and people in general to overcome is the need for "instant gratification," which is prevalent in society today. Instead, a key to success is held in understanding that small incremental changes made over time can produce massive results.

Jasper Blake says: "It's always the small things. It's these tiny little changes over and over and over again, and then a year later, if I look back at videos from a year ago, two years ago, I'm like, oh my gosh, the changes are massive. But none of it happened dramatically... one day it all just worked."

His path to becoming a champion triathlete didn't follow a straight line. He started as a downhill skier, competing through his teenage years at a ski academy in Ontario. But by age 18, his dream of making it to the top levels of skiing began to fade. "It just wasn't happening," he said bluntly. "That was my first real huge setback. I still remember how much it hurt."

Rather than giving up, Jasper pivoted. He picked up tennis, training with the goal of earning a Division I scholarship. It worked. But just as he was finding his footing in college, another passion emerged: triathlon. "I wasn't a natural," he admitted. "But I stuck with it. Perseverance is a muscle—you build it every time you choose not to quit." Years later, that muscle would carry him to the winners' podium in races around the world.

In addition to a willingness to embrace coaching, change, and hard work, one also needs a mindset that can move you forward each day toward your own objectives. Understanding this on a conscious level comes first. At that point, you can begin to internalize and make your new mindset a habit, which I'll get into more later. When you do this, you'll find that getting better is easier, and you will become more resilient to adversity or setbacks.

You may already have already learned in school that resilience also has a biological component rooted in the brain's functionality. In fact, the area that is called our prefrontal cortex, the part of the brain responsible for decision-making and emotional regulation, is absolutely necessary for supporting mental toughness. When athletes face adversity, their prefrontal cortex helps them assess situations, make reasoned decisions, and regulate emotions. And for all of us, staying calm and focused under pressure is critical for maintaining performance during competitions.

Emma Vlasic recounted a pivotal moment in her career. "During a playoff game at Yale, I had a penalty shot to tie the game. I was nervous, but I took a deep breath and repeated my mantra: calm and confident. That mental reset let me focus, and I made the shot. Those two words became my foundation under pressure."

Additionally, the body's stress response system, which involves the release of hormones like cortisol and adrenaline, can impact an athlete's ability to perform. When stress levels are too high, anxiety can impair performance. However, athletes who can modulate their stress response through techniques like deep breathing and mindfulness will handle pressure better and perform at their best.

On this thought, Jasper had shared, "In the early days, I'd let anxiety eat me alive before a race. But I learned to use visualization —not just of winning but of staying calm. I'd picture myself dealing with setbacks in real time. When the race came, I felt prepared for anything."

He had struggled with severe anxiety when he started competing. He was fine during practice, but when it came to competition, he struggled with his emotions. "I was a great skier, technically very good, but really struggled in competitions, mentally not as tough. I think I developed that skill as an athlete in my later years, but as a teenager, I wasn't so good at handling the bigger moments," says Jasper.

Eric Wood says, "We say guys (and girls) who are mentally tough play with emotion, and guys who aren't, play emotionally." It's important to put all your deepest efforts into what you do well, but never let emotions overtake your performance.

Eric explained this brilliantly when he described what he calls the "coffee filter" mindset. "You have to be like a coffee filter and all the information is the coffee grinds. As the water pours through, you're just getting what you want out of it. You don't want all the garbage. You don't want the dirt and the grinds, right? You just want the coffee at the end."

It's essential to use your emotions to play better and not let them get in the way of your performance. We can see this as an example in Michael Jordan. He was a very intense player, but he wouldn't let his emotions impair his play. He had strategies to alleviate his need to express himself in a stressful situation.

In some cases, he'd put on a mean or tough look. Then he would stick his tongue out at another player. He was expressing emotion when doing this, but it wasn't controlling him. Those who struggle let their emotions control them. One bad thing leads to another, into another, and then something really bad might happen. Through these times, we could say that you can talk about being tough or *being mentally tough*.

Understanding the biological underpinnings of resilience can help you harness your brain's power to improve your mental toughness. Scientific research provides compelling evidence for the importance of resilience in sports. Longitudinal studies on athlete development have shown that resilience is a key factor in predicting long-term success.

Such studies follow athletes, tracking their progress and performance to identify the traits and behaviors contributing to their achievements. You may be interested to know that research has found highly resilient athletes to be more likely to achieve their goals and reach higher levels of competition. They are injured less often and are better able to cope with injuries, setbacks, and training demands.

For you as a young athlete, these studies provide valuable guidance about cultivating resilience as one of your foundational skills. I've made sure to include references at the end of this book, in case you want to read more about the studies.

So, how can young athletes like you develop resilience? Several scientifically backed techniques can be woven into your training routines. Effective methods include mindfulness and meditation practices.

These practices help athletes cultivate present-moment awareness, reduce stress, and improve concentration. Regular meditation can also enhance emotional regulation and increase resilience by promoting a calm and focused mindset. Structured mental conditioning exercises are another valuable tool.

These exercises might include visualization techniques, in which athletes mentally rehearse and visualize successful performances (which I'll talk about later), or cognitive-behavioral strategies that challenge negative thoughts and reinforce positive beliefs. In each of the interviews I've done, you'll find that all the athletes used visualization.

How they used such a technique was interesting; Jasper's process was completely different. He said, "I found that visualizing myself in a picture didn't work for me but visualizing what it would feel like worked for me." I'll get into more details about visualization in the coming pages, as it's a very important technique to use and build on as part of your training. By incorporating these practices into your daily routines, you can build the mental resilience needed to thrive in sports and life.

COMMON MYTHS DEBUNKED

Many people think mental toughness is something you're just born with, like having blue eyes or curly hair. But that's a myth. Mental toughness is something you can build and develop over time, just like any other skill. Think about learning to ride a bike. No one is born knowing how to balance on two wheels. You learn through practice, patience, and maybe a few scraped knees.

The same goes for mental toughness. It's not a gift from birth; it's a learned behavior. Studies have proven that anyone can become mentally tough with the proper training and mindset. This is also borne out in the interviews I've done for you. You'll see how each participant built their version of mental toughness, which I'll show you in a moment. This means that no matter where you start, you can always improve. It's about taking small steps every day, facing fears, and pushing boundaries. So, if you've ever doubted your ability to be mentally tough, remember this: It's not a fixed trait but a skill you can cultivate with effort and perseverance.

Another common misconception is that mental toughness means you always have to be positive. Optimism is a great tool, but it's not about ignoring reality or pretending that everything is okay when it's not. Real mental toughness involves realistic optimism. It means acknowledging your emotions, including the negative ones, and dealing with them constructively. Imagine you're a young soccer player who just missed a penalty kick. It's okay—and normal—to feel disappointed or frustrated.

As I discussed a moment ago, the key is not to let those feelings overwhelm you. Instead, allow yourself to feel them, learn from them, and then refocus on the next opportunity. When you accept your emotions, you can address the root cause of what's really bothering you, enabling you to move forward with clarity and purpose. Mental toughness is about resilience, not relentless positivity.

During my interview with Michael Saunders, he talked about how his mother had passed away after a struggle with cancer. He said, "Seeing everything my mom went through, how bad is going 0 for 4 at the plate? Finally, it clicked with me that I gave myself permission to fail; it's okay. Once I did that, the game slowed down for me. I played with a looseness I hadn't been able to play with since I could remember."

You may know about another misguided notion that mental toughness is synonymous with aggression or a lack of empathy. Some believe being tough means being hard and unyielding, but that couldn't be further from the truth. As I discussed with Eric Wood, mental toughness is about maintaining composure and poise, even in the most intense situations. Think of athletes like Roger

Federer, known for his calm demeanor on the court. His ability to stay composed under pressure has been a key factor in his success.

He shows us that you don't have to be aggressive to be tough. Empathy and understanding can be powerful tools in maintaining mental strength. It's about being present, understanding your own emotions, and recognizing the feelings of those around you. This balanced approach fosters solid relationships and a supportive environment, both crucial for long-term success.

And let's talk about the myth that mental toughness is only for elite athletes. Some think you must be a world-class competitor to benefit from mental toughness training. But that's not true at all. Athletes of all levels can develop and benefit from mental toughness. Consider a high school basketball player who starts working on mental strategies before or during practice, such as visualization and positive self-talk.

In my interview with Eric, he talked about Mike Trout, who plays for the LA Angels. "Mike Trout does the same thing he learned his freshman year in high school. When it's his time to walk up to home plate, he takes a huge deep breath, and he has to tell himself something good. Regardless of what it is, he says, 'No matter what, if I'm 10 for 10 or 0 for 10, I do that, and I've committed to it.' That's such a simple thing, but that's his process, which obviously works for him. He's committed. 'It's what's going to make me good,' says Trout."

These tools help him handle the pressure of a big game better, focusing his energy and enhancing his performance. He might not be competing for Olympic gold, but the mental skills he develops will serve him both on the field and in life. The truth is that mental toughness isn't just for the pros. It's for anyone who wants to improve, face challenges with confidence, and grow as an individual. Whether playing in a community league or aiming for a college scholarship, mental toughness is valuable.

Myth-Busting Checklist

- **Myth: Mental Toughness Is Innate**
  - Reality: Mental toughness is a skill that can be developed through practice and effort.
- **Myth: Always Be Positive**
  - Reality: Mental toughness involves realistic optimism, acknowledging and addressing negative emotions constructively.
- **Myth: Toughness Equals Aggression**
  - Reality: True toughness is about calmness and composure, not aggression or lack of empathy. "Play with emotion, but not emotionally," said Eric Wood.
- **Myth: It's Only for Elite Athletes**
  - Reality: Athletes of all levels can benefit from developing mental toughness skills.

THE ROLE OF MINDSET IN SPORTS

Mindset can shape everything you do on and off the field, from approaching challenges to responding to setbacks. It's about seeing challenges as opportunities to learn and grow. When you adopt a growth mindset, you're more open to feedback, more resilient in the face of adversity, and more willing to put in the effort needed to improve. You understand that setbacks are not a reflection of your capabilities but a chance to refine them.

Imagine a young swimmer who approaches every race with a growth mindset. She sets process-oriented goals, focusing on the process and each step she can take in improving her performance rather than just thinking about the outcome. Whether it's refining her stroke technique or improving her starts, she sees each practice as a step toward becoming better.

This approach fosters an environment where learning and development are at the forefront, and performance naturally follows. By concentrating on the process rather than just on the result, she builds a foundation for consistent improvement and mental toughness.

As you read this book, you can follow what you are learning about and redefine your own routine and processes. Trying the practices laid out by successful athletes by doing what they do will help you to also achieve the success that they have experienced.

You will find that the impact of mindset extends beyond your individual performance; it influences how whole teams function and succeed. In a team setting, a collective growth mindset can transform the dynamic, fostering cooperation and shared success. Teams that embrace this mindset view perceive challenges as a chance to come together and innovate.

They encourage each member to contribute ideas and support one another, understanding that their team's success is built on the diverse strengths of its members. Strategies for fostering a collective growth mindset include open communication, celebrating individual and team achievements, and encouraging risk-taking without fear of criticism. Such processes create an environment where everyone feels valued and motivated to give their best.

Cultivating a growth mindset doesn't happen overnight but can be developed with intentional practice. Start by setting process-oriented goals focusing on improvement and effort rather than just results. You'll soon learn to embrace challenges as learning opportunities, understanding they are a natural part of growth.

Reflect on your positive and negative experiences, then consider what you can learn from them. Use language that reinforces a growth mindset, such as, "By focusing on each step of my routine, I get better every day," instead of, "I'm good at this." Surround yourself with people who encourage and support your development. Over time, these practices will help you build a mindset that supports resilience and success.

Later in the book, I'll get specific on how you can create a visualization process for yourself, one that I've used throughout my career.

In the world of sports, mindset plays a crucial role in determining an athlete's trajectory. It's not just about talent or physical ability; it's about how you think and approach your craft. A positive, adaptable mindset opens doors to new possibilities and growth. It allows you to navigate the ups and downs of sports with resilience and determination.

Your mindset will guide you through everything, whether you're facing a tough opponent, dealing with a loss, or striving for a new personal best. By focusing on developing your growth mindset, you're equipping yourself with one of the most powerful tools for achieving success in sports and life.

As you reflect on your mindset, consider how you have handled your experiences over time. Think about your challenges and how your mindset influenced your response. Were there moments when you had a closed mind that held you back? How might adopting a growth mindset have changed the outcome? Use these reflections to guide your approach moving forward, knowing that mindset is a choice you make every day.

Remember what I said at the beginning: "You're in charge of you!" It's about learning from every experience and believing in your capacity to improve, whether quickly or slowly over time. With a growth mindset, you're not just preparing for success in sports; you're setting the stage for a lifetime of learning and achievement.

CHAPTER 2
THE POWER OF ENDURANCE: PUSHING BEYOND LIMITS

 "Champions keep playing until they get it right."

BILLIE JEAN KING

Picture a young runner at the starting line of her first marathon. Her heart pounds in her chest as she recalls the months of grueling training, the days when she felt too tired to continue, and the countless miles she logged alone in the early mornings. Doubt creeps in as she compares herself to the seasoned athletes surrounding her.

Now is the time to be "calm and confident." As the starting gun fires, she remembers she's done the "work" to get her here and why she started this journey—her unwavering passion for running and the dream of crossing that finish line. This is grit in action, which sets successful athletes apart from the rest.

Grit is a powerful force, the mix of passion and perseverance that drives you toward long-term goals, even when the going gets tough. Angela Duckworth, a renowned psychologist, defines grit as the relentless pursuit of your objectives, fueled by an intense passion and a commitment to persevere despite the odds. This means striving toward your goals while sticking to your routine day in and day out, not just when things are going well but especially when they aren't. Grit is about pushing through the inevitable challenges and setbacks that life throws your way. It's the backbone of success in any endeavor, and in sports, it takes an athlete from good to great.

The components of grit are twofold: passion and perseverance. Passion is the driving force behind your commitment, the reason you lace up your sneakers for practice every morning, and why you continue to chase your dream, regardless of setbacks.

It's what gets your heart racing with excitement and keeps you motivated even when you're exhausted. In sports, passion is the love for the game, the thrill of competition, and the joy of personal achievement. Without passion, perseverance fades, and passion alone can wither. On the other hand, perseverance is your ability to keep going, to push through obstacles, and to maintain your effort over the long haul. It's the determination to rise after every fall and the strength to keep striving toward your goals, even when progress seems slow.

Jasper Blake told me, "When I started triathlons, I wasn't a natural. There were moments I fell so far behind I thought about quitting. But I learned that perseverance is a muscle you build by choosing to finish—no matter how ugly the race felt. Over time, that muscle grew, and so did my success."

In the athletic world, grit manifests in every athlete who pushes through tough training sessions, endures injuries, and overcomes failures. We can see this in the swimmer who wakes up before dawn to perfect her strokes, the basketball player who stays after practice to master his free throws, and the runner who tackles hill sprints despite aching muscles. Grit fuels these athletes to keep improving, strive for excellence, and achieve their full potential. As you may also know, sports are filled with stories of athletes who have demonstrated grit. Consider the legendary Michael Jordan, who famously said, "I've missed more than 9,000 shots in my career. I've lost almost 300 games. Twenty-six times, I've been trusted to take the game-winning shot and missed. I've failed over and over and over again in my life. And that is why I succeed." His story is a testament to the power of grit, showing how perseverance and passion can lead to greatness.

Throughout his record-breaking run with the Chicago Bulls, Jordan was known for using his emotions to fuel his game without letting them overwhelm him. Whether it was sticking his tongue out to intimidate an opponent or maintaining his composure in high-stakes moments, Jordan mastered the art of emotional regulation. You'll remember from above how Eric Wood said, "You can play with emotion, but not emotionally."

Eric Wood's journey through the Pittsburgh Pirates organization was defined by adaptability. Originally drafted as a third baseman, Eric soon found himself playing nearly every position on the field. "It wasn't just about where I wanted to play," he said. "It was about what the team needed. You learn quickly that flexibility is as valuable as any skill."

Today, as a coach, Eric focuses on teaching young players not just the technical aspects of baseball but the mental toughness it requires. "I tell them, 'You're going to fail more than you succeed in this sport, and that's okay,'" he shared. "The key is learning how to take that failure and turn it into fuel for the next opportunity."

GOAL ACHIEVING

As a young athlete, you may have already seen people setting and approaching their goals in counterproductive ways. Many people simply say, "Think big," when talking about goal setting.

Eric Wood talked about the importance of writing down his goals: "When I started journaling my progress, it gave me clarity. I'd write things like, 'I'm getting stronger every day,' and I'd visualize myself hitting that new max in the gym. Writing it down made it feel real."

Let's say your big-picture goal is to make it to the professional status of your chosen sport. Focusing on that alone can be counterproductive, because it's too much of a leap from where you are today. However, with that as your goal, there are many steps to get there. What are they? Start by listing them. One sub-goal, or objective, might be making it to your sport's minor or feeder league. But what does it take to get there? What skills do you need to possess? And what does it take to get those skills?

Building physical grit and mental toughness begins with setting long-term goals that fuel your passion and drive. Break these goals into smaller, manageable milestones, and from there, break them down further into daily actionable steps, visualizing each one as you work through this exercise.

Remember what I said at the outset: Develop your own routine and process. This has worked for thousands of people I've taught these techniques to; however, you'll need to adjust them to suit you. First, you must take your goals and break them down into the smallest actionable steps you can do each and every day. A goal without action is just a dream. You must have a step-by-step action plan and track to run on in order to accomplish your goals. Let's look at what I mean.

For each activity and goal, write an affirmation or mantra in the present tense, or, in other words, as if you are doing it.

Here are a couple of examples:

- I am playing in the Major League (use your sport name) by 20xx (pick a realistic date).
- I'm playing in the Minor League by 20xx.
- I'm drafted by 20xx by a Major League team.
- I love taking 200 perfect swings of the bat in a mirror every day.
- I love running three miles every day.
- I love taking 100 ground balls every day.
- Every day, I'm getting batter, I'm stronger and more fit.

Now, this is just a start. Take your daily routine and create similar mantras for each element of it. Once you've done that, you want to review them every morning just after you get out of bed. Do it at this time because your mind is usually more open to receiving your personal programming. Sit down, take a deep breath, and read each line slowly, visualizing it as you read it. I'll talk more about visualization later.

Another method is to record these mantras in your own voice, listen to them each morning, and visualize them happening. I have done this for years, and I can tell you it really works.

The steps above can also be repeated just before going to bed, and I suggest doing this as well. By following this method, you are programming your subconscious mind—on purpose. This helps prevent you from getting distracted. It keeps you focused on your goals and the actions required to get there. You know what you really want to do. Remember, committing to these small daily actions will create major changes over time.

Every day, we are bombarded with messages from external sources, like media, friends and even family on occasion. These messages often don't do us any good and can contradict what we want to accomplish. In order to move ahead on your goals, you must stay focused on your daily actionable steps.

Programming the subconscious mind to achieve goals is a powerful approach. By using daily mantras, you consistently reinforce your positive intentions, gradually influencing your subconscious. As I mentioned before, mantras work best when they are short, powerful phrases written in the present tense.

Repeat this process each morning and evening, and you will be creating habits of success. By doing this, your subconscious goes to work, helping you achieve what you are programming yourself to do. Also, these steps will help you override limiting beliefs or fears that may be blocking your progress. You are embedding new, empowering narratives instead.

Consistency and belief are the keys to success when using this method of developing mental and physical fortitude and toughness. By committing to daily repetition, the subconscious mind adopts these affirmations as truth, building confidence and a sense of inevitability toward your goals.

Over time, you can reshape your self-perception and motivation, making you feel more capable and resilient when facing challenges. By including each activity as a mantra, not only do you know what you need to do each day, but you begin to look forward to doing it with active anticipation.

There are times when you will likely question your ability and whether you "belong." Each of my interviewees expressed this in different ways, which you'll see. The ability to work through those times is critical to your success. Using the technique here will help you.

Right now, no matter where you are in the process, just starting out or almost "there," there are improvements you can make in your game and/or mental toughness, which is why you're reading this book.

You'll also want to know your strengths and weaknesses for the physical side of your development. What routines are you doing now to improve your skills? How many repetitions are you doing? Should you do more? (Probably.) When you approach your workouts, whether on your own or with your team (if you have one), are you practicing purposefully with thought, intension, and intensity? Do you approach each practice to get better in that very same day?

As you set your physical routine, break down each aspect to focus on incremental improvements of each ability required to get better over time. I don't know the specifics of your sport, but I'm sure your coach can help you create it.

This approach makes your goals more achievable and provides a clear path to follow. It's also essential to track what you do and your progress, so you can measure your improvements. By writing about your daily progress, setbacks, and reflections, you gain insight into your strengths and areas for improvement.

As you accomplish the steps, update your affirmations. I've seen this process change people's lives.

This process helps you stay focused, recognize achievements, and maintain momentum. It's also a way to remind yourself of your passion and the reasons you started in the first place.

WRITE IT DOWN TO MAKE IT REAL

Eric Wood said, "The trickiest thing for any young athlete to do is to write it down. I understand we don't need to blog or have a whole notebook, but if you write it down, you can evaluate your outcome."

In your journal, jot down what you did each day to move closer to your goal, any challenges you faced, and how you overcame them. Take a few minutes each week to reflect on your progress and adjust your plan as needed. This exercise is about reaching your goal and developing the grit and discipline required.

Picture this: after a long day of practice, school, and everything else life throws at you, you sit down with a notebook. This isn't just any notebook—it's your space to reflect, unload, and grow. Journaling isn't just about jotting down what happened during the day. It's a powerful tool for self-reflection and personal growth. It helps you become more mindful, bringing awareness to the present moment.

When you write, you process your thoughts and emotions in a way that talking or thinking might not allow. It's like conversing with yourself, where you can explore your experiences and emotions more deeply. Over time, this mindfulness practice helps you understand yourself better, recognize your triggers, and even figure out what truly motivates you.

To get the most out of journaling, consider using different types of prompts to guide your reflections. Start with questions about your daily successes and challenges. What went well today? What obstacles did you face, and how did you handle them? You can write these questions on the first page of your journal for reference. These reflective questions will help you focus on the positives and learn from the negatives.

Incorporating gratitude lists is another fantastic way to keep your mind on the positive aspects of your life. Each day, write down three things you're grateful for. It could be as simple as a sunny day or as significant as a personal victory on the field. This practice trains your mind to see the positive aspects of your life, even on tough days.

While keeping up with your journaling, goal-setting entries are also powerful. This is where you can write your affirmations and have your action plan. Outline your ambitions and break them down into achievable steps. This not only clarifies your path forward but also keeps you accountable.

Journaling doesn't have to be all words. You can incorporate creativity to make the process more engaging and insightful. Try drawing or sketching alongside your written entries. Visual representations of your thoughts and feelings can offer new perspectives. Creating a vision board works for some people as well. Creative expression adds depth to your reflections and can spark new ideas. Clip images and words from magazines that resonate with your aspirations and glue them into your journal or onto a board you put on your wall or desk. It's about making your journal a personal space that reflects who you are and what you want to achieve.

Reviewing past entries is where you'll see the real power of journaling. You'll notice patterns and recurring themes going back through what you've written. Maybe you always feel stressed on game days or notice a boost in confidence after a good practice. Recognizing these patterns helps you understand what works and what needs adjusting. It's also a great way to celebrate your progress.

Look back at where you started and see how far you've come. Each entry is a snapshot of your growth, and over time, these snapshots tell a story of perseverance and development. Celebrate the milestones you've achieved, big or small, because each one is a step toward your goals.

Journaling is more than just a record of events. It's a tool for self-discovery and personal growth. As you write, you'll find clarity in chaos, strength in vulnerability, and direction in uncertainty. It's a practice that enhances your mental game, helping you become more resilient, focused, and aware. So, grab a notebook, find a quiet spot, and let your thoughts flow. Whether you write a sentence or a page, journaling will help you grow as an athlete and a person.

Journaling and affirmations can add to your grit and mental toughness. Grit is not something you're born with; it's something you build through deliberate practice and commitment. By focusing on your passion and persevering in the face of challenges, you can develop the mental toughness, resilience, and determination needed to achieve your dreams. Whether you're an athlete just starting or a seasoned competitor, grit is a trait that will serve you well, both on and off the field.

DEVELOPING SELF-DISCIPLINE

Imagine waking up before dawn, the world still in darkness, as you lace up your skates or shoes. It's not easy to leave the comfort of your bed, but you do it because self-discipline pushes you forward.

At its core, self-discipline is the ability to control your impulses and stay focused on your goals, even when distractions try to pull you off course. It's about finding the right balance between freedom and structure in your life. You need enough freedom to choose and pursue passions, but enough structure to stay on track. For athletes, self-discipline is the backbone of excellence, guiding you through challenges and helping you stick to their commitments, no matter what.

Developing self-discipline starts with establishing daily routines that create habits and set the tone for success. Using your mantras, as I've just talked about, can go a long way in helping you.

Think of your morning rituals as the foundation of your day. Whether it's a quick workout, a nutritious breakfast, or a few minutes of meditation, these routines help prepare your mind and body for the tasks ahead. They create a sense of order and purpose, giving you a head start on the day. It's also essential to prioritize tasks and manage your time effectively. This means identifying what truly matters and dedicating your energy to those activities.

By planning your day, you can avoid the chaos of last-minute decisions and ensure that you're making progress toward your goals. Consistency in your routines creates habits that build momentum, making it easier to maintain discipline even when motivation wanes. Once you've created a new habit or replaced an old bad habit, your success can be virtually automated.

When it comes to creating new habits that will move you forward, one easy trap to fall into is biting off more than you can chew. What I mean by this is that in your excitement to get to where you want to go and "thinking big" in goal-setting terms, you attempt to make an incremental move that is too much for one step in the process. In the fabulous book *Atomic Habits*, James Clear talks about "The Two Minute Rule"; he says, "When you start a new habit, it should take less than two minutes to do."

Seriously, as he further describes in his examples, this means that "studying for class" each day becomes "opening my notes," and "running three miles" five days a week becomes "tying my running shoes." His point and mine are that your efforts and affirmations need to be broken down to the smallest accomplishment to move you forward. Once you master one, to the degree that gives you progress, add another step or make it more complex or difficult.

When you create a habit, you take an activity that you likely think about consciously and turn it into something that you do subconsciously. Doing that makes the activity virtually effortless and allows you to concentrate on the next level you must achieve and the next habit you want to create. Of course, you're likely past the point where you need to tie your shoes; you're already committed, so start from where you are now. Determine what you must do to take your progress to the next level.

But let's be honest: Temptations are everywhere, from the endless scroll of social media to the allure of hanging out with friends instead of hitting the gym. Overcoming these distractions requires conscious effort and strategic planning. Start by reducing screen time and setting boundaries for digital consumption.

Consider using apps that limit your time on social media or simply setting your phone aside during crucial work periods. Recognizing peer pressure and learning to say no when necessary are also essential. A daily workout calendar with times helps many people stay on track. Each entry becomes an appointment, one that you must keep. Surround yourself with people who support your athletic ambitions and understand your commitments. By creating an environment that minimizes distractions, you can focus on what truly matters—your athletic goals.

One quote that stands out as having a significant influence on my business life, which can be applied to your sports, is from a sales instructor named Tom Hopkins. I was in a seminar listening to him, and one of the things he said that I still live by today is:

"Do the most important/productive thing every moment of the day."

This idea holds true whether you're in full workout, school, or relaxation mode. Think about this quote the next time you get to the gym.

Self-discipline is especially vital during training, directly impacting skill development and mental fortitude. Training schedules are designed to optimize performance and ensure steady progress. Adhering to these schedules without deviation is crucial for reaping the benefits of your hard work. This means showing up for practice even when you're tired, giving your best effort, and following through on your commitments. Maintaining nutritional discipline is also essential, as what you eat fuels your body and mind. A balanced diet can enhance performance, speed recovery, and boost overall well-being. By staying disciplined in your training and nutrition, you build a strong foundation for success.

Every athlete knows that the path to greatness isn't always smooth. There will be days when you'd rather binge-watch your favorite show or grab fast food with friends. But it's during these moments that self-discipline truly shines. It's about making choices that align with your goals, even when they're not the easiest or most enjoyable. Think of this process as a muscle that strengthens with use—the more you practice discipline, the more natural it becomes. Over time, the small daily choices add up, setting you on the right path toward achieving your dreams.

THE POWER OF PERSISTENCE

One of my favorite quotes of all time is by Calvin Coolidge on persistence, which is, basically, self-discipline in actionable motion.

"Nothing in this world can take the place of persistence. Talent will not: Nothing is more common than unsuccessful men with talent. Genius will not; Unrewarded genius is almost a proverb. Education will not: The world is full of educated derelicts. Persistence and determination alone are omnipotent."

When you think of an athlete who's made it big, talent is often the first thing that comes to mind. However, talent, while helpful, is not the only ingredient for success. Persistence, the ability to keep going even when things get tough, plays a crucial role in reaching the top. Many athletes have shown us that it's not just about being the most gifted. Take Michael Jordan, for example. He was famously cut from his high school basketball team. Imagine that— a young Jordan, who would become one of the greatest basketball players of all time, was told he wasn't good enough. Instead of giving up, he used this as fuel to work harder, practicing relentlessly to improve his game. This persistence, not just his natural ability, led to his incredible success.

Building persistence is something every athlete can develop, and it starts with setting small, achievable milestones. Think of these milestones as stepping stones on your path to a bigger goal. As I'm sure you can tell, setting goals and forming habits are elements that work together and build on each other. Having just one of the puzzle pieces in place can carry you in your early years, but it takes putting them all together to make it to elite levels. Milestones give you something immediate to aim for and celebrate when you achieve them.

For example, if you're a runner aiming to improve your speed, set a goal to shave a few seconds off your time each week. Each small victory builds your confidence and motivates you to keep pushing toward your ultimate goal. This approach makes significant challenges more manageable and keeps you focused on continuous improvement. It's like that old saying: "How do you eat an elephant?" Answer: "One bite at a time." While I would never suggest, or want, to eat an elephant, I hope you can see the analogy to accomplishing something big. It goes back to doing it incrementally.

Facing setbacks is inevitable in sports, but how you handle them defines your persistence and future. Instead of viewing failures as dead ends, see them as opportunities to learn and grow. This mindset shift can transform how you approach challenges.

Most people will need to make a very conscious decision to shift their mindset. For instance, if you miss a critical shot in a game, analyze what went wrong. Was your form off? Did nerves get the best of you? Use this information to adjust your training, maybe your routine, and come back stronger. Techniques like this help you reframe failures as valuable learning experiences rather than disappointments. They keep you moving forward with a clearer understanding of what needs improvement.

Another real-life example is Serena Williams. One of her most significant challenges came in 2011 when she suffered from a life-threatening pulmonary embolism, followed by additional health complications. This setback forced her to take a break from tennis and fight through an intense recovery process.

Despite these obstacles, Williams returned to the sport stronger than ever, focusing on improving both her mental resilience and physical capabilities. Over the next few years, she went on to win multiple Grand Slam titles, cementing her legacy as one of the greatest tennis players of all time.

Williams often speaks about how overcoming adversity strengthened her resolve and taught her to view setbacks as stepping stones toward even greater accomplishments. Her story is a powerful example of how resilience, mental toughness, and a growth mindset can help an athlete return to form and reach new heights.

Persistence is vital during practice sessions, where repetition and consistency lead to skill mastery. It's not always glamorous, but putting in the hours, day after day, is how athletes refine their techniques and build muscle memory.

Take a musician learning a new song. They don't get it right the first time. They practice each section repeatedly until it flows effortlessly. The same goes for athletes. Whether perfecting a tennis serve or nailing a gymnastics routine, repetition is vital. Through persistent practice, you see incremental improvements, each bringing you closer to mastery.

Keeping enthusiasm high through routine drills can be challenging, especially when progress feels slow. But remember, persistence is about showing up and giving your all, even when you don't see immediate results. Find ways to make practice engaging. Over time, the dedication pays off, and what once seemed difficult becomes second nature.

In sports, persistence is often the decision-maker between those who achieve their dreams and those who fall short. It's the relentless pursuit of improvement, the refusal to quit when things get tough, and the determination to rise after every fall. Talent might get you started, but persistence carries you through the challenges, as Calvin Coolidge says.

COURAGE IN COMPETITION

Courage in sports is like the hidden fuel that propels you forward when the odds are stacked against you. It's not about being reckless or diving headfirst into danger without thought. Courage involves taking calculated risks, understanding the situation, and making decisions that push you beyond your comfort zone while maintaining control.

Picture yourself in your sport or on the soccer field with the score tied and seconds left on the clock. Do you pass the ball, or do you take the shot? Courage is what nudges you to take that shot, trusting in your training and instincts. It's about seizing the moment and making choices that might seem daunting but are necessary for growth and success.

Athletes often face moments where courage is required to make a difference. It might be taking the lead in a critical moment of the game when the pressure is on and everyone is looking at you. Think of the player who steps up to take a penalty kick in a championship match, knowing the outcome rests on their shoulders. Courage also means standing up for a teammate during a conflict and showing solidarity and leadership. It's not always about the big, flashy plays; sometimes, courage is about the quiet, steady actions that inspire those around you. Whether diving for a loose ball, taking charge on the basketball court, or speaking up in the locker room, courageous actions elevate individual and team performance.

Building courage isn't something that happens overnight, and there are exercises and techniques that can help you develop this trait. Visualization is a powerful tool toward this end, which I will talk about in detail. The more you practice visualization, the more confident you'll feel when the moment arrives.

Another technique is gradually exposing yourself to situations that require courage, starting small and building up. This might involve taking on leadership roles in practice, speaking out in team meetings, or challenging yourself to tougher opponents in scrimmages. Over time, these experiences will bolster your confidence and make courageous actions feel more natural to you.

But courage in sports is just the beginning. The skills you develop on the field can translate to other areas of life, fostering holistic personal development in all areas. The courage you build in sports can also empower you to voice your beliefs, stand up for others, and make a positive impact in your community.

This chapter has introduced the building blocks of mental toughness. I have also showed you steps that you can take to develop these qualities in your daily life. Whether it's grit, self-discipline, persistence, or courage, strengthening each trait will contribute to your overall resilience and performance.

CHAPTER 3
THE MIRROR WITHIN: DISCOVERING YOUR STRENGTHS AND WEAKNESSES

 "I had done everything I could've done, and it didn't work out. That was real heartbreak."

JASPER BLAKE

J asper Blake knew he wanted to be an athlete. He reached the top level of downhill skiing. He achieved his goal of getting a scholarship to a Division I university in tennis. Still, he had yet to achieve his pinnacle.

"I want to be an athlete. That was my big thing. That's the only thing I've ever really wanted to do. I recognized early on that the mental side was a problem for me, but I had a hard time doing anything about it until I got into my late teens and early 20s," Jasper said.

As he talks about in the interview, through self-reflection, he recognizes that his emotions and lack of mental control got in the way of his success during competitions. The good news is that Jasper realized this; the bad news is that he didn't know what to do about it. He could only deal with it when he fully understood what was happening in his head. He then went on to be a champion and a professional. His life today is fantastic.

Fortunately, you're reading this book, and the strategies here can help you with the mental part of your game. The difference is that you can learn these strategies even earlier than those who have traveled before you on similar paths as yours.

KNOW YOUR STRENGTHS AND WEAKNESSES

Every athlete has something that sets them apart, a unique ability that makes them stand out. Maybe it's your lightning-fast reflexes or your ability to read the game like a book. Recognizing and celebrating these strengths is crucial. It starts with conducting a thorough personal skills inventory in the areas you need to work on.

Emma Vlasic discovered this while transitioning to college hockey. "At Yale, I realized everyone was fast; everyone was skilled. I had to dig deeper to find my edge. For me, it was my hockey IQ—positioning and reading the game better than others. Once I leaned into that, my confidence soared, and so did my game."

Take a moment to list your core strengths. What aspects of your game come naturally to you? Reflect on past achievements and pinpoint what contributed to those successes. Journaling is a powerful tool here. Write down the moments when you felt most in control—when everything clicked. This reflective practice isn't just about patting yourself on the back; it's about building confidence and self-awareness.

In addition to your evaluation, getting feedback from others is vital to understanding your strengths. Often, you'll find that others can see things from the outside that you can't see yourself. It's not always easy to ask for it, but constructive feedback from coaches and teammates can offer valuable insights.

Once you've identified your strengths and weaknesses, the next step is to leverage your strengths and strengthen your weaknesses. This involves tailoring your training sessions to enhance your standout skills and work on those areas in which you need improvement.

Recognizing these elements of your game is a cornerstone to building mental toughness and confidence. Self-awareness, which stems from understanding your abilities, is a psychological boost. It helps you approach challenges confidently, knowing you have the skills to meet them head-on. Athletes boost their confidence through strength recognition.

One prominent example of an athlete who knows and leverages his strengths to his advantage is Rafael Nadal in tennis. Nadal is famous for his extraordinary endurance, mental toughness, and powerful topspin-heavy forehand. His ability to exploit these strengths is especially evident on clay courts, where he has won the French Open 14 times.

Nadal's stamina allows him to excel in long rallies, often wearing down opponents physically and mentally. His heavy topspin shots give him a tactical advantage, as they bounce high, making it difficult for opponents to attack. Knowing that his left-handed forehand can create uncomfortable angles, he frequently uses it to target his opponent's backhand, forcing them to return high-bouncing balls that are challenging to control.

By strategically mastering and executing his strengths, Nadal has consistently succeeded at the highest level, securing his position as one of the most dominant players in tennis history. You'll also find that by deeply understanding your specific strengths and developing methods to maximize them, you can give you a head start toward building confidence—and winning the game.

EMBRACING WEAKNESSES

Let's face it—recognizing our weaknesses isn't the easiest thing to do. It can feel like spotlighting the parts of ourselves we'd rather hide. But in sports, acknowledging where you need improvement is crucial. It's about looking at your performance with an honest eye, not through a lens of judgment but one of understanding.

Transforming weaknesses into strengths is where the magic happens. It's about turning those steppingstones into platforms for growth. Take a look at some of the greatest athletes in history. Many of them started with glaring weaknesses.

One great example of an athlete who turned a weakness into a strength is NBA star Stephen Curry. Early in his career, Curry was often underestimated because he didn't have the height, size, or strength of a typical NBA player. At 6'2" and relatively slim, he faced doubts about his ability to compete physically with larger, stronger players. However, Curry turned this perceived weakness into one of his most significant assets by perfecting his shooting range and quick release, ultimately revolutionizing the game with his three-point shooting.

Instead of focusing on power, Curry worked on his accuracy, agility, and ability to create shots quickly from any distance. He developed a shooting technique that allowed him to release the ball with incredible speed, making it challenging for defenders to block his shots. He also improved his ball-handling skills, becoming a master at creating space to shoot, even against tight defenses.

By turning what others saw as a disadvantage into a weapon, Curry changed how basketball is played. His deep three-point shooting has forced defenders to cover more of the court, reshaping team strategies across the NBA.

To do this yourself, consider creating a training plan that targets your weak spots. If endurance is your issue, incorporate more cardio sessions. If it's a mental block, perhaps mindfulness exercises could help. Tailor your practice to address these areas consistently. Over time, what was once a weak point can become a defining strength. It's about persistence and the willingness to put in the work where it's needed most.

Embracing your weaknesses doesn't just improve your skills; it builds resilience. The shift from avoiding your weaknesses to accepting and working on them is a powerful psychological change. It fosters a mindset that welcomes challenges rather than shrinking from them.

When you face your weaknesses head-on, you develop invaluable mental toughness. You learn to look at obstacles not as barriers but as puzzles waiting to be solved. This resilience helps you stay calm and focused under pressure, knowing you've faced and overcome difficulties. It's a mental armor that prepares you for whatever comes next, both in sports and life.

Failures related to weaknesses can provide you with some of your most powerful learning moments. They teach you what doesn't work, guiding you toward what does. Consider the story of Thomas Edison, who famously failed thousands of times before successfully inventing the lightbulb. He didn't see these failures as defeats but as lessons that brought him closer to success. In sports, it's the same.

Maybe you lost a game because your defensive skills weren't up to par. Instead of dwelling on the loss, analyze what went wrong and how to improve. Use each failure as a lesson. Many athletes have turned setbacks into comebacks by learning from their mistakes.

It's about facing the aspects of your game that challenge you, understanding them, and working tirelessly to improve them. By doing so, you're enhancing your abilities and cultivating a mindset that sees every challenge as an opportunity for growth. This approach transforms how you view your athletic journey, shifting from focusing on immediate success to incremental improvements over time. The road might be difficult, and the progress might be slow, but each step forward is a victory, bringing you closer to the athlete you aspire to be.

YOUR RAZOR'S EDGE

The Razor's Edge Theory embodies the idea that a slight advantage, even as small as one percent, can decide between success and mediocrity, particularly in competitive sports. However, I don't call it a theory; it is Your Razor's Edge Reality. It's not always grand, sweeping changes that lead to major outcomes but rather the small, consistent, and often overlooked efforts that set apart elite performers. In a field where competition is fierce and the baseline for achievement is already high, the margin between first place and the rest can be razor thin.

Emma: "When you get to the higher levels, it's the small details in your game. It's how you can improve the release of your shot when you're in the moment—because everyone's working hard. Everyone's fast. Everyone's strong."

Eric: "Every athlete is good. They all have the talent. They all have the skill. It's about executing their process."

Understanding and implementing Your Razor's Edge can be transformative as you set yourself apart from others.

The essence of the Razor's Edge Reality is captured in the principle of "small but mighty" improvements. It's about doing just a bit more than someone else. In sports, where peak physical and mental performance is essential, winning and losing often come down to fractions of a second, a few more repetitions, or marginally better techniques.

Athletes who adopt this mindset strive to find and exploit that tiny edge, consistently seeking ways to push just one percent beyond what others are doing. This could mean committing to extra sprints after practice, analyzing game footage for an additional hour, or optimizing nutrition and recovery protocols.

While each effort may seem insignificant, the cumulative impact over time can be monumental. Think of it this way: if your workout routine says to do 100 of X daily, and you do 110 each day instead. It's only 10 more, but that's as much as 70 extra in a week and 3,650 extra per year. How much better can you get with an additional 3,650 reps of X?

One famous example of the Razor's Edge Reality in action can be seen in Olympic swimmer Michael Phelps. His relentless pursuit of perfection went beyond physical training; it included psychological preparation, attention to recovery, and mastering every minute detail of his performance, such as turns and breathing techniques.

The difference between gold and silver at his level could be as slight as a few hundredths of a second. Phelps's dedication to doing just a bit more than his competitors enabled him to accumulate 23 Olympic gold medals, cementing his legacy as the greatest swimmer ever.

This approach can also be applied off the field, inspiring individuals in any field to seek their own one-percent improvements. Whether in the boardroom, classroom, or on the track, the Razor's Edge Reality teaches that the line between ordinary and extraordinary is exceedingly thin. Those willing to push just beyond that line—by doing a little more, learning a bit deeper, and preparing just a bit harder—will find themselves reaping the disproportionate rewards that come from being just one step ahead of the rest. This relentless pursuit of micro-improvement separates the best from the rest and creates champions.

Jasper says: "Are you willing to go into the hurt locker for more than anybody else? That becomes the mental game." What he is referring to when he says this, is your ability to dig deep, work harder and take the extra pain someone else may not be willing to take. Doing this can be part of your Razor's Edge. To stand out in the crowd of athletes, figure out what your Razor's Edge or edges are.. Do them without looking for recognition or praise. These types of actions are usually done in a silent manner with your recognition and payoff being down the road when your talents grow and shine. Doing that little extra will pay off in a big way down the road.

THE IMPACT OF SELF-AWARENESS ON PERFORMANCE

Self-awareness in sports is like having a personal GPS. It helps you understand where you are, where you need to go, and how to get there. It's not about being overly self-conscious, where you constantly worry about what others think. Instead, self-awareness is a clear understanding of your abilities, emotions, and how you respond to different situations. It's the ability to step back and observe yourself honestly and clearly.

For athletes, self-awareness is about recognizing how your body feels during a game, understanding your emotional triggers, and knowing your mental state. This awareness allows you to make informed decisions, adjust your strategies, and improve your performance.

Michael Saunders had excellent success at every level as he went through the ranks playing baseball. However, things changed slightly when he got to the Major Leagues with Seattle. Doubt set in, and his quality was on a downhill slide. After his mother passed away, it was time for a great deal of self-reflection. It was at this moment that his reflection paid off. He said, "Most people would dream to be in my shoes, and I started looking at it like that. My mom had battled and gone through everything that she did; like, why can't I play this game? When you reflect on what is holding you back, whether physical, mental, or both, you can work on any issue you discover.

The benefits of self-awareness extend beyond just knowing yourself better. In the heat of competition, it can significantly enhance your decision-making abilities. Imagine you're a quarterback reading the defense. Self-awareness allows you to recognize your own tendencies and adjust your play accordingly. It helps you stay calm and collected, knowing exactly how you react under pressure. This clarity improves your ability to make quick, smart decisions that can change the outcome of a game. Emotional regulation is another benefit.

When you're aware of your emotions, you can control them instead of letting them control you, as I've already talked about. This means keeping cool when a call doesn't go your way or bouncing back after a mistake. You maintain focus and composure by managing your emotions, which are crucial for peak performance.

Self-awareness also plays a vital role in team dynamics. Self-aware athletes contribute positively to the team environment by understanding their role and how it impacts others. Self-awareness leads to better communication, as you're more attuned to your teammates' needs and emotions. This understanding fosters collaboration, allowing the team to work more cohesively. For example, a self-aware hockey player might recognize when a teammate is struggling and offer support or encouragement.

This empathy strengthens the team bond and creates a supportive atmosphere. By being aware of your strengths and weaknesses, you can position yourself where you're most effective, enhancing the team's overall performance. Self-awareness in teams creates a culture of openness and mutual respect, where each member feels valued and understood.

As you develop self-awareness by consciously observing and evaluating your performance over time, you'll notice its impact on your personal and athletic life. It's not just about knowing your limits but understanding how to push them. It's about recognizing your emotions and channeling them productively.

In sports, self-awareness provides a foundation for growth, allowing you to learn from each experience and improve continuously. Whether you're an individual athlete or part of a team, this skill enhances your ability to navigate challenges, adapt to changing situations, and achieve your goals. Embrace self-awareness as a lifelong practice that evolves and deepens with each game, practice, and reflection.

With a better understanding of yourself, you're equipped to tackle the mental challenges of sports head-on.

CHAPTER 4
YOUR CHAMPION
MINDSET

 "I hated every minute of training, but I said, 'Don't quit. Suffer now and live the rest of your life as a champion."

MUHAMMAD ALI

A champion's mindset might seem hard to understand or describe; however, Kobe Bryant is an outstanding example of an athlete who showcases what a champion mindset can achieve. Known for his "Mamba Mentality," Bryant epitomized relentless dedication, fierce competitiveness, and an unwavering will to succeed. Throughout his 20-year NBA career with the Los Angeles Lakers, he became a five-time NBA champion and one of the greatest basketball players of all time.

Kobe's champion mindset was best displayed during pivotal moments in his career. One defining example was during the 2013 season when he tore his Achilles tendon during a crucial game. Despite the severity of the injury, Bryant demonstrated his incredible mental strength by not only staying on the court but also calmly making two free throws before walking off under his own power. This moment encapsulated his resilience and refusal to succumb to pain or adversity.

Bryant's dedication to continuous improvement served as another testament to his mindset. He was famously known for his rigorous training regimen, waking up at 4 a.m. to practice on his own before team practices even began. His insatiable drive inspired teammates and competitors alike, showing that true champions push beyond their limits to achieve greatness. This was his razor's edge.

Throughout his career, Bryant's champion mindset propelled him to surpass challenges, become a scoring champion, earn MVP honors, and set an example for generations of athletes about what mental toughness, commitment, and hard work can accomplish.

A champion's mindset thrives on adaptability and persistence, which is certainly detailed above. It's about adjusting to new challenges and maintaining focus, even when your path is uncertain. Think of this as mental flexibility, the ability to pivot and find solutions when things don't go as planned; adaptability is coupled with persistence and a relentless drive to keep pushing forward, no matter the obstacles.

Champions view setbacks not as barriers but as opportunities to learn and improve. They understand that success isn't a straight line. It's a journey filled with twists and turns, each offering a lesson that strengthens resolve and determination to succeed.

As you work toward your personal version of a champion's mindset, you will find that continuous learning and improvement become the cornerstones of your achievements. The path is about embracing every experience, both victories and defeats, as a chance to grow.

Champions are lifelong learners, continually seeking ways to refine their techniques and strategies. They're not afraid to ask questions, seek feedback, or try new approaches. This commitment to learning fuels their progress and keeps them at the top of their game. Whether it's studying game footage, analyzing performance, or exploring new training methods, champions always look for that edge that will offer an advantage over the competition.

In learning how to cultivate this mindset, you'll understand that mental conditioning techniques are essential. Goal visualization and mental rehearsals are potent tools that elite athletes use to prepare mentally for competition. Visualization involves creating vivid mental images of successful outcomes, allowing athletes to experience the performance in their minds before it happens. You can also do this: before every training practice and each game. Developing this habit results in building confidence and reducing anxiety, making sporting events feel familiar and achievable.

Establishing a pre-competition mental routine is equally crucial. You might decide that your routine will include specific breathing exercises, positive affirmations, or a series of mental cues that can help you enter a focused and calm state. These techniques prime the mind for peak performance, ensuring that an athlete is ready to perform at their best when the moment arrives.

Before each hockey game, Emma would find a quiet place, take a few minutes to gain focus, and repeat to herself the two words that she lived by, "Calm and confident." Doing this before each game put her in game mode and allowed her to perform to her highest ability. You might wonder how such a simple mantra can help her through the game. First, everyone is different, and depending on your sport, you may need to do something different. There is no right or wrong way; it's all about what works for you.

Integrating mental training with physical practice creates a holistic approach to development. Mindfulness should be combined with your physical drills to enhance focus and awareness during training sessions. Sometimes, you'll want to push yourself beyond how far you feel you can go. Being able to do this will build your champion mindset and mental toughness.

As an example of being mindful, a basketball player might practice by focusing intently on the sensation of the ball as they dribble, noticing the texture and weight of each bounce. This heightened awareness translates to improved concentration during games.

Champion's Mindset Checklist

- **Adaptability**: Practice adjusting your approach when faced with new challenges. Reflect on a recent setback and identify how you could have adapted more effectively.
- **Persistence**: Set a long-term goal and break it into smaller, actionable steps. Track your progress and celebrate small victories along the way.
- **Continuous Learning**: Commit to learning something new each week, whether a skill, strategy, or insight about your sport. Keep a journal of your new knowledge and how it impacts your performance.
- **Visualization**: Spend a few minutes each day visualizing a successful performance. Focus on the details and emotions you want to experience.
- **Pre-Competition Routine**: Develop a routine that calms your mind and prepares you for competition. Experiment with different techniques until you find what works best for you.

STAYING POSITIVE AMIDST CHALLENGES

Staying positive helps you bounce back faster from setbacks and keeps you pushing forward. It reduces stress by shifting focus from what's going wrong to what you can do next.

Michael Saunders shared a lesson in positivity: "When I struck out, I used to get so mad I'd carry it into the dugout. But I learned to flip it. Now, every strikeout is an opportunity to get better. Staying positive is how you keep the game fun."

When you maintain a positive mindset, you open yourself to possibilities and solutions that might go unnoticed. This mental flexibility allows you to adapt and thrive even in the face of adversity.

When you look at athletes who've overcome significant challenges, you'll often find a common thread of positivity. One inspiring example is found in Bethany Hamilton, as a testament to resilience and positivity. At just 13 years old, she survived a life-changing shark attack while surfing in Hawaii, which resulted in the loss of her left arm. Despite this traumatic experience, Bethany's determination and unwavering optimism were remarkable.

Instead of letting fear or frustration take over, she focused on her love for surfing and her faith. Just one month after the attack, she returned to the water, learning to surf with one arm. Her comeback was fueled by her positive outlook, belief in perseverance, and passion for the sport.

Bethany's story of courage and resilience has inspired millions around the world. She became a professional surfer and shared her journey in her autobiography, *Soul Surfer*, which was later turned into a movie. Through it all, she showed that with the right mindset, it's possible to overcome even the most challenging obstacles and become stronger on the other side.

The benefits of cultivating positivity extend far beyond immediate challenges. Over time, maintaining a positive mindset enhances your mental health and well-being. It reduces anxiety and depression, leading to a more balanced and fulfilling life. This positivity also impacts team dynamics. When athletes stay positive, they foster a supportive and encouraging environment, improving collaboration and communication. Positive team dynamics enhance performance and create a sense of camaraderie that elevates everyone involved.

Furthermore, positivity can improve leadership qualities, which you will want to cultivate in yourself as you become stronger in your activities. Positive leaders inspire and motivate their team-mates, leading by example and cultivating a culture of resilience and success. I'll get into this more later when I cover the leadership topic.

How you react to any situation is a choice you can choose to make consciously. However, this is an area in which reacting positively can also be one of the habits you choose to create by repeating the process. This mindset prepares you for the challenges you'll face in sports and equips you with the tools to navigate the ups and downs of life with confidence and grace.

Developing a positive internal dialogue improves your performance and builds mental toughness. It's about creating an inner coach that supports and motivates you, no matter the circumstances.

CHAPTER 5
FOCUSED PRACTICE =
PEAK PERFORMANCE

"It's not how you start, it's how you finish. It's all about the process. Sometimes you can win, but you haven't really gotten better. Other times, you come in second or third, but you know you've improved."

MICHAEL PHELPS

Imagine a young pianist, fingers gliding over the keys, perfecting a piece that once seemed impossible. Her secret? Focused practice. It's not just about playing the same notes over and over—it's about homing in on specific aspects of her performance with intention and precision.

Like mastering a complex musical piece, excelling in sports requires focused practice. It's a concept that exceeds mere repetition, demanding deliberate attention to detail and quality over quantity. In this chapter, you will learn how to practice toward achieving peak performance.

Mike Trout, one of baseball's best hitters, is a master of focused practice. Eric Wood recounted how Trout uses a simple but powerful ritual: 'Before every at-bat, he takes a deep breath and tells himself something positive. It's the same whether he's on a hot streak or a slump. That consistency in mental preparation keeps him sharp.'

Focused practice is a method that targets skill enhancement through intentional and deliberate repetition. Unlike general practice, where the aim might be to put in the hours, focused practice zeroes in on specific skills that need improvement. It's about breaking down complex movements or techniques into smaller, manageable parts and refining them precisely.

Such determined concentration is about something other than mindlessly going through the motions. Instead, it's an active process where each session has a clear purpose, whether perfecting a basketball free throw or nailing the timing of a tennis serve. By concentrating on these targeted areas, athletes can significantly enhance their performance, turning weaknesses into strengths with consistent effort.

The benefits of focused practice are profound. A couple of the most significant advantages are accelerated skill acquisition and mastery. Focusing on specific skills creates neural pathways in the brain that make these actions more automatic and efficient. When you practice this skill, you will realize faster learning results and improved performance.

It's like training your brain to execute the right patterns, making it easier to perform your skills under pressure. Another benefit is improved concentration and precision in performance. Focused practice trains your mind to stay engaged, reducing distractions and enhancing your ability to execute accurately. This heightened concentration boosts your performance and confidence, knowing you've prepared thoroughly for every scenario.

Setting clear and specific goals for each session is crucial to maximizing focus during practice. This means going into practice with a plan, knowing exactly what you want to achieve. Whether improving your sprinting start or perfecting a soccer dribble, having a goal gives your practice direction and purpose.

Mental cues can help maintain concentration. These can be simple phrases or reminders that return your focus to the task at hand. For instance, a swimmer might use the cue "smooth and strong" to focus on their stroke technique. These cues act as anchors, keeping your mind centered on what matters most, especially when distractions arise.

Measuring progress is essential to ensuring that focused practice is effective. This is another area where your journal can come into play and keep you on track. Keeping up your journal through these moments allows you to track your progress. You can also create your plan and make notes on improvements, challenges, and any adjustments made during practice. Review your entries each week to identify patterns, recognize growth, and highlight areas that still need work.

Another method is regularly reviewing video footage of your performance. Suppose you work out with someone on your team; video each other or set up your camera or phone on a tripod. Using video for focused practice can give you accurate insights and allow you to make any needed changes. Watching yourself in action provides valuable insights, allowing you to see exactly what needs improvement.

Creating a video of your performance can also help you with your visualization skills and reinforce other skills you've been focusing on. These techniques keep you accountable and motivate you to continue pushing your limits.

Practice Progress Checklist

- **Set Specific Goals**: Before each practice, write down one or two specific skills you want to focus on.
- **Use Mental Cues**: Create a list of mental cues that help you maintain concentration during practice.
- **Write in Your Journal**: Document each practice session, noting what went well and what needs improvement.
- **Review Video Footage**: Watch recordings of your performance to identify strengths and areas for growth.
- **Reflect and Adjust**: Regularly review your progress and adjust your practice goals as needed.

Incorporating these elements into your routine will make your practice sessions more effective and rewarding, setting the stage for peak performance in your sport and beyond.

CREATING EFFECTIVE PRACTICE ROUTINES

When you lace up your shoes and step onto the field, court, or track, it's not just about the time you put in but how you spend that time. An effective practice routine is about finding that spot between skill development and physical conditioning. It's like building a house; you need a solid foundation, walls, and a roof. In practice, this means dedicating time to honing your technical skills and maintaining your physical fitness. Each session should have a clear purpose, whether it's sharpening your shooting accuracy or boosting your stamina.

But remember, even machines need downtime. Incorporating rest and recovery periods into your routine is crucial. This isn't just about avoiding burnout; it's about giving your body and mind time to absorb what they've learned and letting them come back stronger.

Customizing your practice routine is where the magic happens. It's not a one-size-fits-all approach. You have unique strengths and areas for improvement, and your routine should reflect that.

Personalize your drills to target specific skill gaps. Maybe your footwork needs work, or perhaps your endurance isn't where you want it to be. Modify your drills to focus on these areas, ensuring they align with your overall goals. And remember performance feedback; use it as a guide to adjust the intensity of your sessions. If you're consistently nailing a drill, it might be time to up the challenge. Conversely, if you're struggling, it might be wise to dial it back a bit and focus on mastering the basics.

To gain even more focus, have a strategy to block out all distractions in the room or on the field. Eric Wood says, "The biggest thing for me is sensory deprivation. Take away your senses because your senses are a distraction. Stand in a room with a bat and imagine you're hitting off a pitcher. If it's still difficult, close your eyes and put on some headphones to block out all sound."

Or, if you can, look in a mirror as you practice. Once you like what you see, Eric explains the next step to coaching, "We turn the lights off and then we have them close their eyes." You can do this in your workouts. Then try adding music to help with your tempo. Eric goes on to say, "Sometimes music can help. We incorporate music with a lot of rhythm for those who might struggle with rhythm. We use Beethoven, opera, or music that helps you find the zone and keeps your rhythm on track. There are different strategies." When you're trying a new training routine, such as adding music, try it several times. It will likely feel strange at first, but as you get used to a new strategy, you'll find you can make significant improvements much faster.

Another method Eric talks about is using a metronome for timing. "We like to use a metronome a lot while going through mechanics training for pitchers and hitters. The ability to make adjustments often comes down to the body's timing. We challenge our players by using a fast tempo as well as a very slow tempo. During yoga and other hitting practices, we also use classical music to feel focused and upbeat Hispanic music to feel rhythm" (as communicated by email on October 8th, 2024).

Think of practice time like a budget—finite and precious. To make the most of it, effective time management is key. Prioritizing key drills within limited practice windows ensures you focus on what truly matters. Identify the skills you need that will have the most significant impact on your performance and dedicate your time to them. Using time blocks to concentrate on different skill areas can also enhance efficiency. For instance, dedicate your first 15 minutes to warm-up and conditioning, followed by 30 minutes of targeted skill work, and round off with a cool-down and reflection. This structured approach helps you stay organized and ensures that no area of your training is neglected.

Even when doing focused practice, adding some variety is also important. Incorporating variety not only prevents burnout but also keeps you engaged and motivated. Rotating drills ensures that practice sessions remain dynamic, challenging your mind and body in new ways.

Adding variety could be as simple as switching up your warm-up routine or introducing new drills every few weeks. Integrating competitive elements or mini-games can also add a fun twist. These elements simulate real-game scenarios, testing your skills under pressure and adding a layer of excitement to practice. Participating in a mini-skills tournament with teammates or friends by setting up friendly competitions can ignite that competitive spirit, pushing you to perform at your best. It can also highlight areas where you want to focus your training.

Creating an effective practice routine is both an art and a science. It's about finding what works for you, experimenting, and being willing to adapt. It's about listening to your body and mind, understanding when to push and when to rest, and keeping practice fresh, challenging, and aligned with your goals.

Practice Routine Planner

1. **Skill Development Focus**: Identify one key skill to work on this week. What drills will you incorporate to enhance this skill?
2. **Physical Conditioning**: Choose a physical conditioning exercise to incorporate into your routine. How will it support your skills?
3. **Rest and Recovery**: Schedule rest days or recovery activities (like yoga or stretching). How will you ensure that you adhere to this plan?
4. **Variety Integration**: Introduce a new drill or game to keep your routine dynamic. What will you try this week?
5. **Time Management**: Allocate specific time blocks for each component of your practice. How will you ensure that you stay on track?

This planner will help you create a balanced, effective practice routine that keeps you engaged and on your personal path to improvement.

USING VISUALIZATION TO EXCEL

You'll often hear stories of how professional athletes use visualization to enhance and improve their game. Some also use it, like Michael Saunders, just before stepping into the batter's box. For Jasper Blake, it created the feeling he would experience when he competed. In each interview I must share with you, the pros will talk about how they use visualization. In Eric's early days, he would naturally visualize but didn't yet understand the specifics of what he was doing. "I didn't even know what I was doing, but I was constantly imagining that I was in a situation, whether pitching or hitting." He would do this while watching a live game or one on TV.

Visualization, or mental imagery, is a powerful tool for enhancing performance, focus, and confidence. It involves creating mental images of a desired outcome, such as successfully obtaining a skill or navigating through a competition.

This process is crucial because the mind often doesn't differentiate between actual and imagined events, which means visualizing can activate similar neural pathways as physically practicing. However, while visualization can be transformative, many athletes struggle with it initially, especially if they find it hard to form vivid mental images or maintain focus. Fortunately, like any skill, visualization can be developed and strengthened with practice.

Understanding the Basics of Visualization

Before diving into techniques, it's essential to understand that visualization is more than just seeing something in your mind. It's a multi-sensory experience involving all senses to make the mental image as real and detailed as possible. For athletes, this could mean picturing the court, field, or track, feeling the textures, hearing the sounds, and even smelling the environment. The richer the imagery, the more effective the practice becomes.

Visualization can also take on different forms depending on the individual. Some athletes "see" the image in their mind's eye, while others may "feel" the movements or "hear" the sounds. There's no right or wrong way; the goal is to make it as authentic and engaging as possible for you.

Effective Exercises for Beginners

If you're new to visualization or find it difficult, start small and build up gradually. Begin by finding a quiet place where you won't be interrupted. Close your eyes and take deep breaths to calm your mind. Once relaxed, visualize a simple object, like a ball or an apple. Notice its color, texture, and weight. If you find your mind wandering, don't worry—gently bring your focus back to the image. Practice this for a few minutes each day to improve your concentration.

After practicing with simple objects, start visualizing a basic athletic movement, like dribbling a basketball or swinging a tennis racket. Imagine yourself executing the movement flawlessly. Pay attention to how your body feels, where your hands are, and what it's like to complete the motion. This exercise doesn't need to be long; even a few minutes daily can yield noticeable results over time.

Build Realism and Detail

As your ability improves, you can add more detail and complexity to your mental images. For example, if you're a soccer player, you might visualize dribbling down the field, evading defenders, and scoring a goal. Incorporate as many sensory details as possible—

the sound of the crowd, the feel of the grass, and the sight of the goal approaching. It's important to visualize both the lead-up and the successful completion of the action. This whole process strengthens your mental confidence and prepares you for real-life scenarios.

Troubleshooting Common Challenges

For athletes who find visualization particularly difficult, guided imagery recordings can help you get started. Many sports psychologists and mental performance coaches offer audio files that walk you through a visualization session. You can find apps for your phone that will walk you through the process. Apps like Headspace or Calm offer a range of guided sessions tailored for athletes, making it easy to find a practice that works for you. Listening to a guide can make maintaining focus and engaging all senses easier. Another effective strategy is to practice visualization right after physical training. At this time, your body and mind are already primed for the sport, and it can be easier to recall sensations and movements.

Consistency is Key

Like any skill, consistent practice is the key to improving your visualization ability. Start with just five minutes a day, gradually increasing the time as it becomes easier. Visualization can be as valuable as physical practice for many athletes, helping build confidence, resilience, and readiness. By committing to these exercises regularly, you'll find that visualization becomes a natural and effective part of your mental training toolkit, leading to improved performance and mental toughness on the field.

MEDITATION IN SPORTS

Picture this: You're on the starting line, heart racing, mind buzzing with thoughts of the competition ahead. It's easy to feel overwhelmed in moments like these. This is where meditation steps in, offering calm amidst the storm. Meditation is about training your mind to focus, calm down, and stay present. It's not just for yogis or monks; it's also a powerful tool for athletes.

Mindfulness meditation, for instance, is about being fully aware of the present moment, which helps you tune out distractions and focus on the task at hand. Then there's transcendental meditation, a technique that involves silently repeating a mantra to help you dive deeper into relaxation, which reduces stress and anxiety. Both meditation forms can significantly enhance your athletic performance, allowing you to approach your sport with a clear, focused mind.

The benefits of meditation for athletes are immense, touching both the mind and body. On the mental front, meditation enhances focus and concentration, which are crucial during competitions. Regularly practicing meditation trains your brain to maintain attention, even when pressure is high. This mental discipline helps you stay in the zone, easily making split-second decisions. Moreover, meditation reduces anxiety and improves emotional regulation. It provides a mental reset, helping you manage nerves before a big game or bounce back from mistakes quickly. On a physical level, meditation can enhance your body's response to stress by lowering your heart rate and relaxing tense muscles. This holistic approach to training boosts performance and promotes overall well-being.

Incorporating meditation into your routine might seem daunting initially, but it doesn't have to be. Start with guided meditation sessions that focus on visualization. These sessions involve imagining your success, seeing yourself executing skills flawlessly, and feeling the emotions associated with victory. Visualization in meditation reinforces positive outcomes, making them feel achievable. Another technique is using breathing exercises to calm pre-competition nerves. Simple exercises like deep belly breathing help slow your heart rate and ease tension.

Before a game, take a few minutes to breathe deeply, inhaling through your nose and exhaling slowly through your mouth. This practice calms your mind and centers your body, preparing you for peak performance.

Creating a consistent meditation routine is key to reaping its benefits. Start by setting aside a specific time each day for meditation, even if it's just five minutes. The morning can be a great time to meditate, as it sets a positive tone for the day. Use meditation apps or resources to guide your practice, providing structure and variety. Consistency is more important than duration, so focus on making meditation a regular part of your routine. Over time, you'll notice its impact on your focus, resilience, and overall mindset.

Incorporating meditation into your daily life creates a mental edge that enhances your athletic abilities. It's about more than just performance; it's about developing a mindset that supports your growth, both on and off the field. As you explore meditation, remember that it's a personal journey. Find what resonates with you, experiment with different techniques, and be patient with yourself. Like any skill, meditation takes practice, but its rewards are well worth the effort.

FOCUS UNDER PRESSURE

Pressure. It's the invisible opponent every athlete faces, as real as any competitor standing across from you. In the world of sports, pressure comes from all angles. Coaches expect you to execute the perfect strategy, teammates rely on you to perform your role flawlessly, and spectators anticipate a thrilling performance. Then there's the internal pressure—the goals you set for yourself, the aspirations that drive you to excel.

These expectations, while motivating, can also feel like a heavy weight on your shoulders. They can blur your focus and make even the simplest tasks seem monumental. Understanding this pressure is the first step in learning how to manage it. Recognize that it's a part of the game. Rather than letting pressure hinder you, use it to fuel your performance.

In high-pressure situations, staying focused and calm is paramount. In each interview, you'll see how each athlete talks about the importance of remaining calm during competition. One effective strategy is mental rehearsal. Picture yourself in challenging scenarios, whether taking the final penalty kick or executing a complex routine. Visualize each detail, from the sounds to the movements, as if you're there. This mental preparation will help you build confidence and familiarity, making the event feel like another practice session.

Another key strategy is developing a pre-competition focus routine. This could be a series of actions or thoughts that center your mind. Maybe it's listening to a particular song, repeating a motivational mantra, or doing a warm-up exercise. This routine becomes your anchor, a reliable way to calm your mind and sharpen your focus before the big moment.

Distractions are inevitable in any sport, but overcoming them can give you a significant edge. During competitions, your mind might wander, or external factors may disrupt your concentration. In these moments, techniques for refocusing are crucial. One method involves pausing briefly, taking a deep breath, and resetting your attention.

Grounding yourself can bring your focus back to the present task. Creating mental anchors can also help, such as cues or reminders that pull you back into the moment. It might be a specific word, a touch of a lucky charm, or even a brief visualization of your goal. These anchors serve as focal points, helping you maintain concentration in the middle of chaos.

Building resilience to pressure is about transforming it from a source of stress into a motivator for peak performance. Use pressure as a driving force, a challenge that pushes you to reach your full potential.

Reflecting on past experiences is a powerful tool in this process. Think back to times when you faced pressure and succeeded. What strategies did you use? What mindset helped you prevail? By analyzing these experiences, you can build a mental toolkit that prepares you for future challenges. This reflection boosts your confidence and reinforces your ability to handle pressure effectively. Emma Vlasic says, "Once you get into those situations, you can adapt quicker, especially at the moment when you've already thought it through in your head."

She reflected, "My first year at Yale, I had no confidence. I'd sit on the bench and question if I even belonged there. But I started repeating two words to myself—calm and confident—before every game. Those words built me back up and helped me play like I belonged."

Building resilience also involves a shift in mindset. See pressure as an opportunity to showcase your skills rather than a threat. It's about embracing the moment, trusting in your preparation, and giving your best effort. This positive mindset fosters confidence, enabling you to thrive despite high stakes. Remember, every athlete experiences pressure. What sets the greats apart is how they respond to it. By developing strategies to maintain focus and build resilience, you can turn pressure into an ally rather than an adversary.

It's clear that mastering your mental game is just as important as physical prowess. These will tools enhance your performance and prepare you for the many challenges sports and life throw your way.

CHAPTER 6
WHY FAILURE FUELS SUCCESS

 "Confidence is such a big, big part of it, and I didn't have that confidence the first year and a half of playing."

EMMA VLASIC

Earlier, I wrote about Emma's story and how she took the challenges of her first year and a half on the Yale hockey team and turned that experience from struggling to captain of the team. She could have folded or quit and not made the extra effort to turn things around. Struggles come in many forms, and it's rare, if not unrealistic, for an athlete to not experience setbacks. Your attitude around the challenges is often separates those who go on to greatness from those who get cut from the team. When setbacks occur, treat them as the beginning of something greater. Here's the secret that many successful athletes know: Failure is not a dead end. It's a stepping stone, a critical feedback form that can propel you to new heights. Understanding how to view failure through this lens can transform your approach to sports and life.

Failure is a natural part of the learning process. It's like a teacher that shows you what needs improvement. Without it, growth stagnates. Think of it as learning to ride a bike. Those initial falls were crucial—they taught you balance, coordination, and persistence. In sports, failure operates similarly. It highlights areas that require refinement, allowing you to hone your skills. It's not just a setback when you miss a shot or lose a match; it's a chance to analyze what went wrong and how you can improve. This perspective shifts failure from a negative experience to a valuable opportunity for skill enhancement.

Adopting a positive mindset toward failure is key to unlocking its potential. Instead of seeing setbacks as roadblocks, view them as opportunities for growth. Celebrate the small successes embedded within failures.

Perhaps you lost the game but executed a new move perfectly or maintained excellent communication with your team. These actions are victories in themselves, worthy of recognition. By focusing on these positives, you cultivate a mindset that embraces challenges and fosters resilience. Embracing failure with a growth mindset helps you stay motivated and committed to continuous improvement, turning each setback into a stepping stone toward success.

Analyzing failures is an essential skill that can help you identify areas for improvement. Start by breaking down performance errors into specific components. Was your timing off? Did you misjudge the distance? Look for patterns and triggers that frequently lead to mistakes. You may notice that nerves affect your performance in high-stakes situations or that fatigue sets in during the final minutes of a game. Understanding these patterns allows you to address the root causes and prevent future errors. This analysis is not about self-criticism; it's a constructive process to refine your skills and strategies. Then, take what you've discovered and create a focused training plan around it.

Creating a feedback loop is a powerful way to use failure as a tool for growth. Incorporate feedback from coaches and peers, who can offer valuable insights into your performance. Set up a system to track and reflect on your improvements.

Keep a journal where you document each game, noting what went well and areas that need work. Regularly review this journal to track your progress over time. This feedback loop transforms failure into a dynamic learning experience, guiding your practice and strategy adjustments. It keeps you focused on development, ensuring that each setback contributes to your advancement.

Failure Analysis Exercise

- **Reflect on a Recent Setback:** Write about a recent failure in your sport. Describe what happened, how you felt, and what you learned from the experience.
- **Identify Key Learnings:** Break down the event into specific elements. Note what went wrong and what went right. Identify patterns or triggers that contributed to the outcome.
- **Set Improvement Goals:** Based on your analysis, set specific goals for improvement. What skills need refining? What strategies can be adjusted?
- **Create a Feedback Loop:** Commit to seeking feedback from coaches or teammates. Use their insights to inform your practice and track your progress over time.

Recognizing failure as feedback can be a game-changer. It fosters an environment of learning and growth, where each mistake becomes a lesson and every setback catalyzes improvement. By embracing this approach, you unlock the potential within each failure, using it to fuel your journey toward success in sports and beyond.

BOUNCING BACK: RESILIENCE IN ACTION

Resilience is the backbone of mental toughness, enabling athletes to withstand and recover from setbacks. In sports, resilience is the ability to bounce back from failure, adapt to challenges, and emerge stronger. It's what separates those who crumble under pressure from those who rise to the occasion. Resilient athletes display perseverance, adaptability, and an unwavering belief in overcoming obstacles. They understand that setbacks are temporary while the path to success is rarely linear. This mindset empowers them to keep pushing forward, regardless of their challenges. Developing resilience is not just about enduring tough times; it's about growing through them.

Building resilience starts with developing a supportive network of peers and mentors who can offer guidance and encouragement. Surrounding yourself with individuals who understand your goals and challenges creates a safety net that catches you when you stumble and pushes you to keep going.

Mentors can provide valuable insights and share their own experiences of overcoming adversity, offering a roadmap for navigating challenging situations. Additionally, setting realistic, incremental goals for recovery is crucial. These goals provide a sense of direction and purpose, allowing you to track progress and celebrate small victories along the way. They break down seemingly insurmountable challenges into manageable steps, making the journey to recovery feel achievable.

Resilience can be cultivated through specific exercises and activities designed to enhance mental strength. Journaling about past challenges and your responses to them can be incredibly insightful.

By reflecting on how you've handled difficulties before, you gain clarity on your strengths and identify areas for improvement. Writing about these experiences also helps you to reinforce lessons learned and builds confidence in your ability to handle future setbacks. Another effective exercise is simulating high-pressure scenarios during practice. You can practice staying calm and focused under stress by recreating the conditions of a real game or competition. This preparation equips you with the tools needed to maintain composure when it matters most, reinforcing your resilience in the face of adversity.

Real-life stories of athletes who have demonstrated incredible resilience can be powerful sources of inspiration. Consider the journeys of professional athletes who faced career-threatening injuries. At the peak of their career, everything came crashing down with a single misstep. But instead of giving up, they embraced the challenge, dedicating themselves to rehabilitation and complete recovery. Through sheer determination and resilience, they returned to their sport and achieved new heights of success.

Another example might be an athlete who experienced repeated failures in their quest for victory. Each loss was a blow, but they used it as fuel to work harder, refine their skills, and eventually triumph over their competitors.

You can find these stories at nearly any bookstore and also online. Such stories highlight the transformative power of resilience, showing that setbacks can catalyze remarkable achievements.

Resilience Reflection

Consider the following questions to reflect on your resilience:

Think about a time when you faced a significant setback in your sport. How did you respond, and what did you learn from the experience?

Who are the people in your life who support and encourage you during challenging times? How can you lean on them to help build your resilience?

What small, realistic goals coupled with action steps can you set to help you in your recovery from a recent challenge? How will you celebrate each step forward?

Reflecting on these questions helps you identify your resilience strengths and areas for growth. It reminds you that resilience is not just about enduring difficulties but also about learning and thriving through them.

LEARNING FROM MISTAKES: A PRO ATHLETE'S PERSPECTIVE

Many professional athletes, including the four featured in this book—Jasper, Eric, Emma, and Michael—offer a treasure trove of wisdom about learning from mistakes. These individuals, who have reached the pinnacle of their sports, have faced their fair share of blunders and setbacks. Yet, instead of letting them define their careers, they use them as learning opportunities.

For instance, LeBron James has spoken about how early career losses taught him resilience and the importance of preparation. He often says that each loss is a lesson, a chance to analyze what went wrong and how to improve.

Similarly, Serena Williams emphasizes embracing mistakes, seeing them as stepping stones rather than stumbling blocks. Her approach is to understand the errors, learn from them, and move forward with renewed determination. Such insights are invaluable, showing that even the most outstanding athletes view mistakes as part of their growth.

Analyzing mistakes is a crucial technique that professional athletes use to improve, and you should too. One common method is video analysis of competitive situations, if it's available. This visual feedback allows you to pinpoint specific areas that need work, such as technique, timing, or positioning. Watching a play unfold on a screen can allow you to pinpoint mistakes that aren't always apparent in the heat of the moment. Consider reflective sessions with coaches and mentors. These discussions offer a chance to talk about what happened, gain new perspectives, and brainstorm solutions. Coaches can provide objective insights, helping you see things that you might have overlooked. This collaborative approach ensures that learning from mistakes becomes a constructive process, leading to tangible improvements.

Case studies of athletes who have learned from their mistakes offer powerful examples of what's possible. Here are two examples:

1. **Tom Brady** – When Tom Brady entered the NFL, he was drafted in the sixth round and was seen as an underdog. To gain an edge, he relied heavily on watching game films. Brady became known for his meticulous study of game footage, analyzing his own plays and those of his opponents. This video analysis allowed him to identify defensive tendencies, improve his decision-making, and refine his mechanics. His dedication to studying film turned what others saw as average physical skills into the foundation of his success, leading him to become a seven-time Super Bowl champion and one of the greatest quarterbacks in history.

2. Serena Williams – Throughout her career, Serena Williams used video analysis as a critical tool to improve her game. After tough losses or subpar performances, she would meticulously review her matches to understand what went wrong and identify areas for improvement. By studying her opponents' patterns and her own weaknesses on video, she could adjust her strategy and sharpen her skills. This dedication to video analysis helped her evolve, maintain her dominance, and win 23 Grand Slam singles titles, solidifying her legacy as one of the greatest tennis players ever.

These stories demonstrate how athletes can turn mistakes into triumphs through dedicated effort and strategic adjustments.

Applying lessons learned from mistakes is the final step in this transformative process. For many athletes, this means adjusting their training regimens based on the patterns identified in their mistakes. The key is to remain open to change and be willing to adapt. Athletes who successfully learn from their mistakes view each one as an opportunity to refine their skills and elevate their performance. They understand that mistakes are not failures; rather, they are part of the journey to becoming a better athlete. This mindset makes all the difference—turning setbacks into setups for success.

As you navigate the ups and downs of your athletic career, remember that setbacks are not the end of the road. They are the beginning of new opportunities waiting to be discovered. By embracing this mindset, you transform your challenges into valuable lessons, equipping yourself with the tools needed to succeed both on and off the field.

CHAPTER 7

PERFORMANCE ANXIETY AND STRESS MANAGEMENT

 "Your mind is your strongest tool or your weakest link. How you choose to use it can shape your reality."

KERRI WALSH JENNINGS

S imone Biles, one of the greatest gymnasts in history, is a powerful example of overcoming performance anxiety to reach incredible heights. In 2021, during the Tokyo Olympics, Biles experienced a highly publicized struggle with performance anxiety, known as the "twisties"—a mental block that disrupts spatial awareness and makes high-level gymnastics moves dangerous. With the world's eyes on her and immense pressure to add more medals to her already impressive collection, Biles made the bold decision to withdraw from multiple events to prioritize her mental health.

This moment was significant because of its rarity. It showcased the reality that even the most accomplished athletes are not immune to performance anxiety. Instead of seeing this as defeat, she worked through her anxiety by focusing on mindfulness, breathing techniques, and stepping back to reconnect with her love of the sport without overwhelming expectations.

By addressing her anxiety head-on, Biles returned to competition later in the Games and won a bronze medal on the balance beam. This achievement represented far more than a medal. Biles's experience inspired countless athletes and fans, showing that overcoming performance anxiety isn't just about pushing through but understanding when to step back, regroup, and come back stronger.

Performance anxiety can creep in for many reasons. Often, the fear of failure looms large, casting a shadow over your confidence. You might worry about letting your team down or not meeting the expectations of coaches, parents, or yourself. These thoughts can lead to a cascade of physical symptoms—your heart races, your breathing quickens, and you might even feel your stomach churn. Emotionally, you might experience self-doubt or an overwhelming urge to flee from the pressure. If you let this all in to your experience, the combination of physical and emotional responses can derail your focus. Still, the good news is that there are ways to manage this anxiety and turn it into a positive force.

Jasper Blake said, "My body understands how to move, but my brain was always getting in the way."

One effective strategy for managing pre-game jitters is establishing a pre-competition ritual. As I've said, Emma would take some time pre-game and tell herself to be "calm and confident." Michael Saunders would visualize the pitcher throwing him a pitch that he's "barrel up" each time he entered the on-deck circle. These rituals can be incredibly grounding, giving you a sense of control when everything else feels unpredictable. Some athletes find solace in music, curating a playlist that pumps them up or calms their nerves. Others might have a lucky jersey or a specific pair of socks they wear every game. The power of these rituals lies in their ability to create a mental trigger—a signal to your brain that it's time to focus and perform.

Mental preparation is another crucial component of overcoming anxiety. Like Michael, visualization is a powerful tool that can help you mentally rehearse your performance. Alongside visualization, positive affirmations can reinforce your sense of self-belief. Simple statements like "I am ready" or "I trust my training" can shift your mindset from doubt to determination.

A swimmer I once knew had a similar approach. Before each race, he would sit quietly, close his eyes, and visualize himself gliding through the water. He imagined the rhythm of his strokes, the feel of the water, and the crowd's cheers as he touched the wall first. This visualization not only boosted his confidence but also helped him manage the anxiety that used to overwhelm him. By mentally preparing before the race, he transformed his nerves into a source of energy, propelling him to success.

Pre-Game Ritual Checklist

- **Create a Playlist:** Choose songs that either energize or calm you. Listen to them as you prepare for your competition.
- **Lucky Item or Routine:** Identify a lucky item or establish a consistent pre-game routine that signals your brain to focus.
- **Visualization Practice:** Spend a few minutes each day visualizing a successful performance. Engage all your senses for the most impact.
- **Positive Affirmations:** Write down affirmations that resonate with you. Repeat them before each game or practice to boost your confidence.

These rituals and mental strategies are your tools to tackle pre-game jitters. They're about calming nerves and setting the stage for peak performance.

BREATHING TECHNIQUES FOR CALMNESS

Eric Wood: "When players are stressed, they're often shallow breathing. When you're experiencing mental stress, your heart rate jumps, but your muscles don't need oxygen. If anything's going to change, you have to slow your heart rate back down to have better cognitive ability, and then you see that you have perspective."

One powerful technique is diaphragmatic breathing, which Michael talks about using. Diaphragmatic breathing, commonly referred to as "deep breathing" or "belly breathing," engages the diaphragm—the large, dome-shaped muscle located at the base of the lungs. This breathing method promotes more efficient oxygen intake and deeper lung expansion compared to shallow, chest-level breathing. In sports, diaphragmatic breathing plays a crucial role in enhancing both physical and mental performance.

As you continue on with your sporting journey, you may learn that the primary advantage of diaphragmatic breathing is its ability to maximize oxygen intake, ensuring that muscles receive sufficient oxygen to sustain prolonged periods of physical activity. This increased oxygen flow helps delay the onset of fatigue and supports quicker recovery, making it essential for endurance sports such as running, cycling, and swimming. By improving your oxygen delivery, you can maintain peak performance for longer durations, which translates to better results.

Another critical benefit of diaphragmatic breathing is its impact on stress management and focus. You have likely experienced high-pressure scenarios in sports, such as competition or critical game moments. These situations can trigger our body's fight-or-flight response, causing rapid, shallow breathing and increased heart rate. This is exactly when you want to practice a new breathing technique and make it into a habit.

The best way to counter our potential for a fight-or-flight response is to engage in diaphragmatic breathing, which stimulates what is called the vagus nerve. This nerve activates the parasympathetic nervous system, inducing a state of calm and reducing stress levels. Athletes who practice this technique regularly report enhanced concentration, improved mental clarity, and greater control over their performance.

Diaphragmatic breathing can also help you with core stability and posture. By training your diaphragm, you can strengthen your core muscles, contributing to better balance, reducing injury risk, and improving overall physical performance. Whether in high-intensity sports like basketball or precision-based activities like archery, diaphragmatic breathing will equip you with a powerful tool to enhance both your physical capacity and mental resilience, making such a breathing method an essential part of every comprehensive training regimen.

Instead of breathing shallowly from your chest, you can breathe deeply into your diaphragm. To practice, sit or lie down comfortably. Place one hand on your chest and the other on your belly. Inhale deeply through your nose, allowing your belly to rise as it fills with air. Exhale slowly through your mouth, feeling your belly fall. Repeat this for a few minutes and notice how it brings a sense of calm and clarity.

Another effective method is box breathing, also known as the 4-4-4-4 method, which enhances concentration and control. It's called "box" breathing because each breath phase is like a side of a box of equal length. Start by inhaling through your nose for a count of four. Hold your breath for four counts.

Exhale slowly through your mouth for another four counts, then hold your breath again for four counts. This structured approach to breathing helps regulate your body's stress response, making it easier to focus and stay calm under pressure. Try practicing box breathing when you're feeling anxious or distracted and see how it sharpens your concentration.

Eric Wood uses this method with his players to calm and slow their heart rates. He says, "It's four fours. You take a deep breath in for four seconds. You hold it for four seconds. You breathe out for four seconds, and you do that four times." Eric then mentions that his players wear heart rate monitors, so each player can watch recovery time and see how the stress of a workout is affecting the player.

Incorporating breathing exercises into your routine is easier than you think. Consider starting each practice session with a few minutes of diaphragmatic breathing. This sets a calm tone, helping you transition from whatever's been on your mind to being fully present. During practice, take short breathing breaks to reset your focus. If you feel your mind wandering or frustration building, pause and take a few deep breaths. This simple act can work wonders for your concentration and performance.

Let's look at how athletes utilize breathing techniques in high-pressure moments. A tennis player, for example, might use breathing to stay centered between serves. As she steps up to the line, she takes a deep, deliberate breath, calming her nerves and clearing her mind. This ritual becomes a way to reset her focus, allowing her to approach each serve with renewed precision. Similarly, a basketball player might employ breathing during free throws. Standing at the line, he takes a deep breath, releases it slowly, and visualizes the ball swishing through the net. This routine helps him block out distractions and maintain composure, even with the game on the line.

Breathing techniques are like a secret weapon, accessible to anyone willing to practice them. They don't require fancy equipment or hours of training, just a few moments of mindfulness. Making breathing practice a regular part of your routine creates a solid foundation for mental and physical resilience. Whether preparing for a big game or navigating everyday stress, these techniques offer a reliable way to find calm and focus through the storm.

GROUNDING EXERCISES FOR FOCUS

Imagine you're in the middle of a high-stakes game. The noise, the expectations, the adrenaline—it can all be overwhelming. This is where grounding exercises come into play. Grounding is about returning your mind to the present moment, a technique that can help maintain focus and reduce anxiety. It cuts through the noise, pulling you back from the whirlpool of intrusive thoughts and distractions. When you ground yourself, you're anchoring your attention to the here and now, making it easier to concentrate on your performance. This isn't just about ignoring pressure; it's about acknowledging it and directing your focus elsewhere.

There are several grounding techniques you can use to center your-self. Sensory grounding is one approach. You engage your senses to anchor your awareness to your immediate environment. For instance, take a moment to notice the ball's texture in your hands, the sound of your cleats on the grass, or the rhythm of your breathing. These sensory cues can pull you out of your head and into the present, where you have control.

On the other hand, physical grounding involves simple movements that connect you to your body. You might clench and unclench your fists, tap your toes rhythmically, or take deliberate steps to feel the earth beneath you. These actions remind you of your physical presence, steering your mind from spiraling thoughts.

Incorporating grounding exercises into your practice and competition routines is straightforward and effective. During warm-ups, consider setting aside a few moments to engage in sensory grounding. Focus on your surroundings—the colors, the sounds, the smells. This practice calms your nerves and sharpens your awareness, making you more attuned to the game.

Timeouts or breaks offer another opportunity to apply grounding strategies. When the game pauses, use that time to center yourself. Engage in physical grounding by shaking your arms or rolling your shoulders to release tension. This quick reset can differentiate between a scattered mind and a focused one.

Athletes across various sports have found grounding exercises to be invaluable tools. Take, for example, a soccer player who struggled with maintaining focus after making a mistake on the field. Instead of dwelling on the error, he learned to use sensory grounding techniques. He would quickly focus on the feel of the grass under his feet or his teammates' voices, bringing his attention back to the game. This practice allowed him to regain his composure and continue playing with clarity and purpose.

Similarly, a track athlete found grounding exercises essential before settling into the starting blocks. By focusing on the sensation of the track beneath her spikes and the sound of the starter's gun, she could block out distractions and hone her focus on the race ahead.

These grounding techniques offer practical solutions to the mental challenges you may face. They're not just quick fixes but valuable skills that enhance your performance and overall well-being.

By anchoring yourself in the present, you reduce the power of anxiety and distractions, giving yourself the freedom to perform at your best and enjoy the moment. Grounding exercises, when practiced regularly, become second nature, a reliable part of your athletic toolkit. Whether it's the sensory cues that connect you to the environment or the physical movements that ground you in your body, these techniques provide a pathway to focus, resilience, and success on the field, track, or court.

Through grounding exercises, you gain more than just a focus strategy. You develop a deeper connection to your sport, the sensations that define it, and the moments that make it meaningful. Each grounding exercise reminds you that while the game may be intense, your ability to focus is always within reach.

MANAGING EXPECTATIONS AND PRESSURE

Pressure is a constant companion for athletes, whether from external expectations of coaches, parents, and fans or internal pressure from personal goals and aspirations. Imagine a young soccer player eager to impress on the field and in the classroom while juggling the expectations of family, friends, and themselves. It's a lot to carry; sometimes, it feels like a heavy weight pressing down. This pressure can be motivating but can also lead to stress if not managed well. Understanding the sources of this pressure is the first step in learning how to navigate it.

It's easy to feel like you're not just playing for yourself but for everyone else, too. This can be overwhelming, especially when you're already pushing hard to achieve your goals. Internal pressure is just as challenging. You set high standards for yourself, aiming to reach a personal best or secure a spot on the varsity team. These aspirations are important but can become burdensome when they lead to self-doubt or anxiety about not measuring up.

To manage these expectations, it is helpful to frame them as opportunities for growth rather than as insurmountable challenges. Instead of viewing a coach's critique as a judgment, consider it a chance to improve your skills. Each piece of feedback can be a stepping stone toward becoming a better athlete. Setting realistic and achievable performance goals is another effective strategy.

Building resilience to pressure is crucial for thriving in high-stakes environments. Simulating high-pressure conditions during practice can prepare you for the real thing. For instance, create scenarios with high stakes, like practicing a penalty kick with teammates watching, mimicking the pressure of a game situation. These drills teach you to stay calm and composed, no matter the circumstances.

Consider the story of a young golfer who faced the intense pressure of tournament play. For her, managing expectations was about focusing on her game rather than the leaderboard. She learned to treat each hole as a new opportunity, concentrating on her swing and breathing rather than the score. This shift in focus allowed her to play with freedom and joy, ultimately leading to better performances. Remember what Michael said, "Once I gave myself permission to fail, the game slowed down for me. I played with just a looseness that I hadn't been able to play with since I could remember."

These strategies for managing expectations and pressure are about reducing stress and embracing the challenges of being an athlete. By reframing expectations, setting achievable goals, and building resilience, you can transform pressure into a catalyst for growth. This approach not only enhances your performance on the field but also equips you with valuable skills in all areas of life.

YOUR ACTIVATION LEVEL

When dealing with anxiety and stress, the moment prior to completing is very important. I've given examples already, but knowing your optimum activation level is also very important and often overlooked.

The activation curve in sports refers to the relationship between an athlete's level of arousal (or mental and physiological readiness) and their performance. It's a concept derived from the Inverted-U Theory, which suggests that performance improves with increased arousal up to an optimal point. After this peak, too much arousal can lead to anxiety, muscle tension, and decreased focus, causing a drop in performance.

Here's a breakdown:

- Low Activation: At low arousal, athletes may feel relaxed or even bored. They lack the energy and alertness needed for optimal performance, resulting in slower reaction times and less intense engagement.
- Optimal Activation: With moderate arousal, athletes reach their "zone" where they are alert, focused, and confident. This is the peak of the curve where performance is at its best—often referred to as the "flow state."
- High Activation: When arousal exceeds optimal levels, performance can suffer due to over-activation. Symptoms like racing thoughts, tension, and decreased coordination or focus can arise, pushing athletes into a state where they're overstimulated, which can lead to mistakes.

The ideal activation level varies by sport, position, and individual athlete. For example, a gymnast may need lower arousal to maintain balance and precision, while a sprinter or mixed martial arts fighter benefits from high arousal for maximum explosive power.

Determining your place on the activation curve requires a mix of self-awareness, experience, and, sometimes, guidance from coaches or sports psychologists. Athletes can learn to recognize where they fall on this curve by observing their mental and physical responses during training and competition. Here are some methods you can use to pinpoint and adjust your activation level:

1. **Self-Assessment of Physical and Mental Cues**
    o   **Physical Cues**: Notice signs like muscle tension, heart rate, sweating, and breathing patterns.
    o   **Mental Cues**: Mental states such as confidence, focus, and alertness also give you clues. If you feel overly anxious, jittery, or distracted, you may be beyond the optimal activation point. Conversely, feeling too relaxed or sluggish indicates that you are under stimulated.
2. **Journaling and Performance Tracking**
    o   Using a journal here can give you insights into your pre-performance feelings and post-performance outcomes, so you can start identifying patterns. Record your physical and emotional states before, during, and after events, noting when you have performed best. Over time, this can reveal where you need to be on the activation curve for optimal performance.
3. **Experimenting with Activation Techniques**
    o   You can experiment with routines that increase or decrease arousal, such as:
        ▪   **Increasing Activation**: Listening to upbeat music,

performing fast-paced warm-ups, or using self-talk can raise arousal levels.

- **Decreasing Activation**: Deep breathing, visualization, and meditation help lower arousal for sports that demand calmness and precision.

o You can gauge the effectiveness of these techniques for you and adjust them as most helps you, based on your needs.

4. **Feedback from Coaches and Teammates**

o Coaches often observe an athlete's body language, energy levels, and execution. They can provide insights as to how you perform at various arousal levels.

5. **Practicing Under Varied Conditions**

o Try to simulate different arousal levels in practice by adjusting external conditions, such as practicing with distractions, under time pressure, or in quiet, controlled settings. This can help you understand your performance with different activation levels and identify techniques for hitting their "sweet spot" effectiveness at game time.

Through these practices, you can become more in tune with where you need to fall on the activation curve personally, given your temperament and sport. Understanding these methods and developing strategies to reach your ideal arousal level for consistent peak performance can be part of your razor's edge.

The bottom line is that learning how to control your stress and anxiety while remaining calm but strong will go a long way toward helping you at all levels of your game.

CHAPTER 8
NUTRITION AND LIFESTYLE FOR MENTAL TOUGHNESS

 "Proper nutrition is key to sustaining my peak performance. If I know I'm fueling my body correctly, it makes me mentally tougher too. The discipline and focus on what I eat reflects on the field."

TOM BRADY

I magine you're on the field, the sun blazing, sweat trickling down your face, and your heart pounding. You've trained for months, honing your skills and pushing your limits. Still, there's something else playing a crucial role in how you perform today—nutrition. You might not see it, but what you eat can make or break your game. Nutrition isn't just about fueling your body; it's about fueling your mind, too. It's the hidden powerhouse behind your cognitive performance and mental resilience. Let's dive into how the proper nutrients can boost your mental game, helping you stay sharp and focused when it matters most.

NUTRITION'S ROLE IN MENTAL PERFORMANCE

Understanding nutrition's impact on cognitive functions and mental resilience is like unlocking a secret advantage in sports. Your brain, much like the rest of your body, relies on a steady supply of nutrients to function optimally. The food you consume directly influences your brain's ability to process information, make decisions, and maintain focus during high-pressure moments. Diets rich in essential nutrients enhance neurotransmitter production, a chemical messenger that facilitates communication between nerve cells.

This communication is vital for maintaining mental clarity and emotional stability, especially when under stress. Ensuring a balanced diet isn't just about physical performance—it's about equipping your brain to handle the mental demands of competition.

Critical nutrients for brain health play a pivotal role in supporting your mental acuity. Omega-3 fatty acids found abundantly in fish, like salmon, and plant sources, like flaxseeds, are crucial for brain function. They help build cell membranes in the brain, improving cellular communication and enhancing cognitive performance. Antioxidants in colorful fruits and vegetables, like berries, spinach, and carrots, protect brain cells from damage caused by free radicals.

These antioxidants aid in reducing inflammation and oxidative stress, both of which can negatively impact mental performance. Incorporating a variety of these nutrient-rich foods into your diet gives your brain the tools it needs to stay sharp and resilient.

Meal planning for athletes requires a strategic approach to ensure that both physical and mental performance are optimized. Balancing macronutrients—proteins, carbohydrates, and fats—is essential. Proteins help repair and build muscle tissue, supporting recovery and growth.

Carbohydrates are your body's primary energy source, fueling your workouts and keeping your brain alert. Fats, especially healthy ones like those from avocados and nuts, are vital for long-term energy and brain health. It's crucial to time your meals around training sessions to maximize energy levels and mental sharpness. Eating a balanced meal 2–3 hours before training provides the necessary fuel without weighing you down, while a light snack 30–60 minutes before exercise can give you an extra energy boost.

Hydration is another critical factor in maintaining cognitive function and focus. Dehydration can lead to decreased concentration and impaired physical and mental performance. When you're dehydrated, your brain has to work harder to perform tasks, leading to fatigue and reduced mental clarity.

To stay hydrated, make it a habit to drink water consistently throughout the day, not just during workouts. Carry a water bottle with you and set reminders to take sips regularly. Consider incorporating hydrating foods like watermelon, cucumbers, and oranges into your meals and snacks. These strategies ensure that your brain remains well-hydrated, allowing you to maintain focus and perform at your best.

There is a large variety of hydrating mixes you can add to water during strenuous workouts. There are also liquid drinks like Gatorade and others. Essentially, these are meant to replace electrolytes that you sweat out of your body to maintain a balance in your system. Other drinks or supplements are specifically for recovering after your workout.

Understanding and applying nutritional principles can enhance your mental toughness, giving you an edge in sports and life.

Nutrition is not just a supporting player; it's a crucial component of your overall performance strategy, empowering you to think clearly, react quickly, and stay resilient despite any challenges.

Do some research, and if you have access to a nutrition coach on your team or otherwise, consider a consultation to set you up with a regime that is right for you.

MEAL PLANNING & SUPPLEMENTATION

Take a moment to plan a day's worth of meals that incorporate the key nutrients discussed. Think about breakfast, lunch, dinner, and two snacks. How can you include omega-3s, antioxidants, and balanced macronutrients? Write down your plan and consider how you can adjust your current eating habits to better support your physical and mental performance.

Adding the right nutritional supplements can be valuable to your meal plan, enhancing performance, recovery, and overall health. However, approach supplementation carefully and prioritize safe, effective options based on your individual needs and sport-specific demands.

Firstly, ensure that your diet is balanced, as supplements cannot replace a well-rounded meal plan. Consult with your nutritionist to tailor choices based on age, sports intensity, and dietary gaps. Commonly recommended supplements include protein powder, which supports muscle recovery and growth, and electrolytes, which help replenish essential minerals lost through sweat during intense training sessions. Omega-3 fatty acids can reduce inflammation, and vitamin D benefits bone health, especially for athletes training indoors or in colder climates.

Additionally, choose certified products tested for purity and banned substances, as contaminated supplements can risk an athlete's career. Reading ingredient labels and avoiding excessive doses of vitamins and minerals is key to preventing adverse effects. By strategically adding supplements with a nutritionist or other professional, you can optimize your nutrition and enhance performance without compromising your safety or health.

SLEEP'S ROLE IN RECOVERY

Imagine finishing a grueling practice, your muscles sore and your mind exhausted. You hit the pillow, and as you drift into sleep, your body begins its remarkable work. Sleep is the unsung hero in your recovery process when your body repairs and strengthens itself. During deep sleep, growth hormones are released, aiding in muscle repair and growth. This is crucial for all athletes who push their physical limits. Your body struggles to recover without adequate sleep, leaving you tired and more susceptible to injuries. But it's not just your muscles that benefit from a good night's rest.

Sleep plays a significant role in mood regulation, helping to stabilize emotions and keep irritability at bay. Think about those days when you wake up grumpy after a restless night. That's your brain telling you it didn't get the rest it needed to recharge. This mood stabilization is vital, especially when juggling sports, school, and social life pressures.

Creating an environment conducive to quality sleep can make a world of difference in how you feel and perform. Start by establishing a consistent sleep schedule, going to bed and waking up at the same time every day, even on weekends. This routine helps regulate your body's internal clock, making it easier to fall asleep and wake up feeling refreshed. Reducing exposure to computer or phone screens before bedtime is another powerful strategy.

The blue light emitted by phones, tablets, and computers can interfere with your body's melatonin production, the hormone responsible for regulating sleep. Try setting a screen curfew on yourself an hour before bed and opting for calming activities like reading or listening to music instead. Creating a calm, dark, and quiet sleep space also helps your brain associate your bedroom with rest, signaling it's time to wind down.

Napping can be a game changer for athletes, offering a quick performance boost and alertness. Short naps, especially those lasting 10 to 30 minutes, can enhance mental clarity without leaving you feeling groggy. Timing your naps is crucial to reaping the benefits—early afternoon is ideal, as it complements your body's natural circadian rhythm. These power naps can improve reaction times, help consolidate learning, and enhance memory, making them an excellent tool for athletes looking to sharpen their mental edge. However, napping too late in the day or for too long can disrupt your nighttime sleep, so finding a balance that works for you is essential.

Recognizing the signs of sleep deprivation is key to addressing and preventing it. Inadequate sleep can manifest in various ways, impacting your mind and body. You might notice increased irritability and mood swings, affecting how you interact with teammates and coaches.

Decreased reaction times and focus during competitions can also occur, leading to mistakes and a lack of sharpness on the field. These symptoms are your body's way of signaling that it needs more rest to function optimally. If you find yourself experiencing these issues, it may be time to reassess your sleep habits and make adjustments to ensure you're getting the quality rest you need. Remember, sleep is not a luxury for athletes; it's a critical compo nent of your training regimen, just as important as the hours you spend practicing or the meals you eat.

Consider implementing a bedtime routine with relaxation techniques like deep breathing or gentle stretching. These practices can help calm your mind and prepare your body for sleep. If you regularly have a hard time falling asleep or other sleep issues persist, consulting a healthcare professional or sleep specialist may provide insights and solutions tailored to your specific needs. Prioritizing sleep and recovery enhances your athletic performance. It supports your overall well-being, allowing you to stay on top of your game physically and mentally.

BALANCING SPORTS, SCHOOL, AND SOCIAL LIFE

Managing the whirlwind of sports, school, and a social life can feel like juggling flaming torches. Each one demands your attention and dropping one can lead to chaos. So, how do you keep everything in the air without getting burned out? It starts with effective time management strategies. Using planners or digital tools can be a game changer.

Whether it's a classic paper planner or a scheduling app like Google Calendar, having a visual overview of your commitments will help you to stay on top of everything you need to do. Blocking out time for practices, study sessions, and social activities keeps you organized and prevents last-minute scrambles. It's about being proactive rather than reactive.

Set boundaries to avoid overcommitment. If you're spread too thin, everything suffers. So, learn to say 'no' when necessary, even if it's tough. This isn't about missing out but prioritizing what's important to you. When you write it down in your calendar, treat each activity like a "must-attend" appointment unless there's an emergency; you have set a commitment to yourself.

Creating a balanced routine is crucial for maintaining harmony between your athletic, academic, and social pursuits. Allocate dedicated time for study and training, ensuring neither is neglected. This might mean hitting the books right after practice or waking up early to squeeze in a workout before school. While it sounds intense, having a routine makes these transitions smoother and less stressful.

Scheduling social activities is just as important. Time with friends isn't just fun; it's necessary for mental health. Whether it's a movie night or a simple catch-up over lunch, these moments recharge you. And don't forget personal downtime—reading a book, listening to music, or just relaxing. These activities, though seemingly minor, help maintain your mental equilibrium. Write them all on your calendar; this discipline supports your mental toughness.

Recognizing the signs of imbalance is key to maintaining this balance. Burnout and stress aren't always easy to spot when you're in the thick of it, but there are telltale signs. It might be time to reassess your commitments if you are constantly tired, irritable, or anxious.

Physical symptoms, like frequent headaches or trouble sleeping, can also indicate stress. When these signs appear, it's crucial to recalibrate. Take a step back and evaluate your schedule. Are you over-committed? Is there a particular area that's taking too much of your time? Once you identify the issue, adjust accordingly. Maybe it's dropping an extracurricular activity or asking for help with schoolwork. Remember, it's okay to make changes to protect your well-being. It's about playing the long game, not just surviving the day-to-day grind.

Communicating your needs effectively is a skill that can significantly ease the pressure. Open dialogues with coaches, teachers, and family members are essential. If you're struggling to balance everything, let them know. They can't help if they don't know there's a problem.

Negotiating deadlines or expectations can relieve some of the stress. A coach can adjust practice times, or a teacher might offer an extension on an assignment. Building a support network is equally important. Friends, family, and mentors can provide both emotional and logistical support. They can help with transportation and study sessions or offer a listening ear when you need to vent. This safety net makes it easier to tackle the challenges of balancing multiple priorities.

CREATING A SUPPORTIVE ENVIRONMENT

Having a solid support system is like having a secret weapon in sports. It's not just about what happens on the field or court; it's also about the people who cheer you on from the sidelines and lift you up when you're down. A supportive environment can differentiate between a good athlete and a great one. Positive reinforcement from coaches and peers plays a huge role in this. When a coach acknowledges your hard work or a teammate praises your effort, it boosts your confidence and motivation. This kind of encouragement reinforces the belief that you can achieve your goals, no matter how tough the competition gets. It's like having a personal cheer squad that fuels your drive to keep pushing forward.

Family involvement is another crucial aspect of a supportive environment. When your family invests time and effort into your sports journey, it creates a sense of unity and purpose. Family support is invaluable, whether it's attending games, helping with early morning practices, or simply being there to listen after a tough day. It provides stability and a sense of belonging, reminding you that you're not alone in your pursuits. This involvement teaches valuable life lessons about teamwork, commitment, and resilience. Knowing that your family believes in you can be a powerful motivator, encouraging you to give your best effort in every practice and competition.

Emma had this to say about her parents, "They've been very supportive and just also allowing us, my two brothers and I, to figure out our own path."

Eric said, "We made the decision as a family that I was going to go to Pickering High School because they had a baseball coach that took it more seriously, who had practices before and after school."

Building a positive team culture is essential for fostering mental and emotional well-being. A team that encourages open communication and mutual respect creates an environment where athletes can thrive. It's essential to celebrate team and individual achievements collectively, recognizing the hard work and dedication to reaching those milestones. This collective celebration builds camaraderie and strengthens the bond between teammates. When athletes feel valued and appreciated, they are more likely to support one another and work together toward common goals. A positive team culture also helps athletes navigate challenges and setbacks, providing a safe space to learn and grow without fear of judgment. "Team first" is how to think about successes as you build your skills and advance through the ranks.

Sometimes, athletes may need to seek external support to navigate mental or emotional challenges. Recognizing when professional help is needed is also an important skill. As you advance, you'll find most teams now have "performance coaches," who help with the mental part of the game. If feelings of stress, anxiety, or burnout become overwhelming, consulting with a mental health professional or sports psychologist can provide valuable insights and coping strategies.

These experts can help athletes develop mental resilience, manage pressure, and improve performance. Accessing resources for mental support should be viewed as a strength, not a weakness. Just as you would seek medical attention for a physical injury, addressing mental concerns is crucial to maintaining overall well-being and achieving peak performance.

Mentorship is another powerful tool in an athlete's development. Having mentors in sports and life opens opportunities for guidance, support, and valuable insights. Mentors serve as role models, offering advice and sharing their experiences to help you navigate challenges and make informed decisions. Finding someone who inspires and motivates you can be transformative, whether it's a coach, an older teammate, or a family friend. Learning from mentors' experiences and insights can help you develop your skills, build confidence, and set ambitious goals. Mentorship also fosters a sense of accountability, encouraging you to stay focused and committed to your aspirations.

In sports, a supportive environment is a crucial ingredient for success. It's about surrounding yourself with people who believe in you, challenge you, and celebrate your achievements. It's about creating a culture that values teamwork, communication, and mutual respect. And it's about recognizing when to seek help and finding mentors who can guide you.

These elements work together to build a foundation of mental toughness and resilience, empowering you to achieve greatness in sports and life. The people around you are there to lift you, cheer you on, and help you reach your full potential.

CHAPTER 9
TRAIN YOUR MIND THROUGHOUT THE DAY

> *"We'll take thousands of reps and hundreds of hours, but people struggle to spend ten minutes a day on strengthening their mind. Your mind is a muscle just like every other muscle in your body where you can make it strong."*

MICHAEL SAUNDERS

Every athlete has that moment. The alarm rings, and you lie in bed, fighting the urge to hit snooze. Your calendar is packed with practice, school, and social commitments. Still, you also know that today holds the potential for greatness. The key to unlocking this potential lies in the routine you set for yourself. Establishing a daily mental toughness routine is like sharpening a tool you'll use every day. It's not just about the physical grind; it's about training your mind to be as fit and resilient as your body. These daily drills are your secret weapon, your razor's edge, preparing you to face challenges confidently.

One powerful way to kickstart your mental toughness routine is by setting morning focus rituals and reviewing your written mantras and visualization. Imagine starting each day by setting a daily intention, a simple commitment to yourself about what you want to achieve. This goes beyond just visualizing your goals, as I talked about. Setting your intentions is like giving your day a roadmap. It aligns your actions with your goals, helping you navigate distractions and remain focused. Pair this with a few minutes of breathing exercises. Take deep, calming breaths to center yourself, letting go of any anxiety about the day ahead. This practice not only wakes up your body but tunes your mind for the tasks ahead of you.

As the day winds down, it's time to reflect. Evening reflection helps you process the day's events, acknowledging achievements and challenges. Consider what went well and what could be improved. Did you meet your morning intention? What obstacles did you face, and how did you handle them? This reflection isn't just about critiquing yourself; it's about celebrating your successes and learning from your experiences. It's a practice that builds self-awareness and resilience, allowing you to approach each new day with a fresh perspective and renewed determination.

Short, impactful exercises are the backbone of maintaining consistency without feeling overwhelmed. These exercises are designed to fit into your busy schedule, taking no more than 10 minutes but packing a significant punch.

Incorporating variety into your routine keeps the mind engaged and prevents monotony. Rotating through different exercises, such as mindfulness, visualization, and self-talk drills keeps things fresh. Mindfulness helps you stay present, reducing stress and enhancing focus. Visualization reinforces positive outcomes, while self-talk boosts your confidence and motivation. Each exercise targets a different aspect of mental toughness, creating a comprehensive training regimen for your mind.

As I've discussed, tracking your progress is crucial for staying motivated and seeing how far you've come. Using your journal to log your daily exercises, reflections, and achievements can keep you focused and help you track your progress. By monitoring your progress, you create your own feedback loop that reinforces positive habits and encourages continuous improvement.

SPORT-SPECIFIC MENTAL EXERCISES

In the world of sports, one size definitely does not fit all. Each sport comes with unique challenges, requiring specific physical and mental exercises to hone the skills you need for success. Take soccer, for instance. It's not just about physical prowess; it's about reading the game, anticipating moves, and working seamlessly with teammates.

Role-playing scenarios are another powerful tool. They allow you to simulate real-game situations, developing quick decision-making skills. Gather your teammates and run through pressure-filled scenarios.

Maybe it's a sudden-death penalty shootout, a bottom-of-the-ninth inning with bases loaded, or a buzzer-beater situation. Practicing your mental responses to these unexpected events helps you develop the calmness and clarity needed to make split-second decisions. It's about preparing your mind to react precisely and confidently, even when the stakes are high.

Evaluating the effectiveness of these sport-specific mental exercises is essential. Track your performance metrics before and after implementing these exercises. Are you making more successful plays? Do you feel more confident and composed during games? Anecdotal evidence, like personal experiences or competition results, can provide insight. Reflect on how these mental exercises have impacted your performance. Have you noticed a particular improvement in your focus or decision-making? Use these observations to fine-tune your mental training, ensuring it supports your growth and success as an athlete.

DEVELOPING YOUR PERSONAL PLAYBOOK

Imagine having your own secret weapon, a tool tailored just for you that enhances your mental game. This is your personal playbook, and creating one is what this book is about. It's a unique guide with strategies and exercises crafted to boost your mental toughness. It can be part of your journaling process, or your playbook can be something separate. Think of it as a compilation of your favorite mental exercises and routines that resonate with you and keep you grounded. Your playbook is where you can jot down personal mantras and affirmations—words that motivate you to push through the tough days. It's not just a collection of tips; it's your mental toolkit, personalized to fit your needs and ambitions.

Creating this playbook is about more than just writing down exercises. It's about customizing its content to give you your razor's edge and to align with your strengths, weaknesses, and goals. Start by identifying the sport-specific drills and exercises that you find most effective.

Maybe it's a visualization technique that helps you prepare for big games or a breathing exercise that calms your nerves before a match. Include these in your playbook, ensuring they reflect your unique challenges and motivators. As you set personalized goals, note them in your playbook. This keeps you accountable and allows you to track your progress over time. Your playbook becomes a living document, evolving with you as you grow and develop.

Using your playbook during practice and competition can reinforce your mental toughness. It serves as a quick reference for pre-game routines and focus techniques, helping you stay centered and prepared. Before a game, flip through your playbook to review your goals and affirmations. Your playbook will become a tool for preparation and growth, helping you continuously improve.

It's important to remember that your journal and/or playbook is not static. It is updated almost daily to reflect your growth and changing needs. As you gain new insights and discover new strategies, incorporate all of this into your playbook. Adjust your focus based on evolving goals and achievements. By keeping your playbook current, you ensure that it remains a relevant and effective tool. It's a personalized guide that grows with you, adapting to your changing landscape as an athlete.

As you fill your playbook, consider the bigger picture. It's not just about individual exercises or routines, but it's about creating a comprehensive resource that supports your mental training. Your playbook is a testament to your commitment to mental toughness. It reflects your dedication to becoming the best version of yourself, both on and off the field. As you move forward, keep this playbook by your side. Let it guide you through challenges, motivate you in moments of doubt, and celebrate your successes.

CHAPTER 10
THE CRITICAL ROLE OF PARENTS AND COACHES

"The best advice for young athletes is to have fun, enjoy the game, and make friends along the way. Parents and coaches should focus on fostering that joy rather than just the wins. When kids love the game, that's when they truly excel."

WAYNE GRETZKY

Picture yourself on the sidelines of a little league game, the air buzzing with the excitement of young athletes ready to give their all. Parents and coaches stand together, eagerly watching the action unfold, each uniquely shaping the budding sports stars in front of them. This chapter discusses how parents and coaches can effectively support young athletes, creating an environment that fosters growth, learning, and confidence. It's about understanding the importance of communication and how it can be the key to unlocking an athlete's potential, helping them navigate the highs and lows of their athletic journey.

COMMUNICATING EFFECTIVELY WITH YOUNG ATHLETES

Building open lines of communication is foundational for any supportive environment. It's about creating a space where young athletes feel safe to express themselves without fear of judgment. Regular check-ins can be a game-changer. These don't have to be formal meetings; they can be as simple as a conversation on the car ride home from practice. The goal is to discuss progress and challenges in a way that encourages openness; active listening is crucial. It means hearing what your athlete is saying and paying attention to their words, tone, and body language. It's about responding thoughtfully, showing that you value their thoughts and feelings. This builds trust, making it easier for them to share what's on their mind, whether it's a concern about their performance or a personal issue.

Encouraging honest feedback is another pillar of effective communication. Young athletes should feel comfortable voicing their thoughts and feelings without fear of criticism. This requires setting a tone of respect and empathy in all interactions. When an athlete shares a concern, respond constructively. Instead of dismissing their feelings or immediately offering solutions, acknowledge their perspective. Use phrases like, "I understand why you feel that way" or "Let's explore this together." This approach fosters a sense of validation and empowerment, encouraging them to continue sharing openly. It's about creating a dialogue where both parties feel heard and respected, leading to more meaningful and productive conversations.

Communication styles should be adaptable to suit the individual needs of each athlete. Recognize that everyone has a unique way of processing information and expressing themselves. Some athletes may respond better to visual aids or demonstrations, while others prefer verbal explanations or written instructions. Tailoring your communication method to match their learning style can significantly affect how they understand and retain information. It's about being flexible and willing to adjust your approach to ensure clarity and understanding. This customization shows your young athletes that you are invested in their growth and willing to meet them where they are, which fosters a more supportive and effective learning environment.

Navigating difficult conversations is an inevitable part of supporting young athletes. Whether discussing performance issues or addressing personal setbacks, these conversations require care and compassion. Start by empathizing with sensitive topics, acknowledging the athlete's feelings, and providing reassurance. It's helpful to develop scripts or key points to guide the conversation, ensuring you address all necessary aspects without overwhelming the athlete.

Focus on the facts and avoid placing blame; instead, frame the discussion around improvement and growth. For example, if an athlete struggles with a particular skill, discuss strategies to help them overcome this challenge. Offer encouragement and support, reinforcing their potential and commitment to progress. When handled with care, difficult conversations can lead to breakthroughs in understanding and improvement.

Encourage athletes to keep a journal, as discussed earlier in this book. Their journal serves as a private space for reflection, helping them to articulate their experiences and identify areas they want to discuss. It can also be a conversation starter during check-ins, providing a reference point for athletes, coaches, or parents. By documenting their journey, athletes gain insight into their progress, challenges, and evolving goals, fostering self-awareness and confidence in their ability to communicate effectively.

ENCOURAGING GROWTH WITHOUT PRESSURE

Finding the balance between encouragement and pressure is a tightrope every coach and parent must navigate. Picture an athlete standing on this rope—on one side lies motivation and growth, and on the other, stress and burnout. Too much pressure, and you risk tipping the balance into anxiety and disengagement. It's crucial to recognize signs of stress early; perhaps the athlete seems unusually tired, withdrawn, or less enthusiastic about practice. These could be red flags indicating burnout. Instead of focusing solely on winning, emphasize progress and effort. Celebrate improvement in techniques, dedication to practice, and resilience shown in challenging games. This shift in focus reduces pressure and fosters a more supportive environment. It allows athletes to thrive, knowing their efforts are valued regardless of the outcome.

Michael Saunders says, "I promised myself that I would never live vicariously through my kids, and I never have expectations of them. I give them the freedom and the opportunities to open and close their own doors. You can't make a child want it. They either have that competitive fire, or they don't, and that's okay."

Setting realistic expectations is another key component. This involves understanding an athlete's current abilities and setting goals that stretch them without overwhelming them. Work together to set both short-term and long-term goals. Short-term goals focus on mastering a specific skill. In contrast, long-term goals involve broader aspirations like making the varsity team. The important thing is that these goals are collaborative, reflecting the athlete's interests and capacity. Adjust these expectations based on feedback. If an athlete expresses feeling overwhelmed, consider recalibrating. It's about creating a path that encourages growth while respecting the athlete's well-being. This approach promotes ownership and keeps athletes engaged and motivated, knowing they have a say in their development.

"My goal was to get a scholarship, and I got one with a Division 1 school," said Jasper.

Celebrating small victories is not just about the big wins. It's about recognizing each step forward, no matter how small. These moments of acknowledgment can be powerful motivators.

Organize team or family celebrations for reaching milestones, like a personal best in a race or successfully learning a new skill. These celebrations don't need to be grand. A simple acknowledgment in front of teammates can make an athlete feel appreciated and motivated to continue striving. Verbal affirmations are equally important. A coach's "Great job on that drill today!" or a parent's "I'm proud of how hard you're working" can go a long way in building confidence and reinforcing effort.

Michael says about his children, who are athletes, "I don't forget how hard the game is. I just tell my kids how much I love watching them play the game and try to build their confidence that way."

Fostering intrinsic motivation is about nurturing a genuine love for the sport that comes from within. It's the difference between playing because you love it and playing because you feel you have to. Encourage athletes to reflect on their motivations and passions. Ask them, "What do you love most about playing?" or "What excites you to train?" These reflections help athletes connect with their intrinsic motivations, reinforcing their love for the game. Create opportunities for self-directed learning. Give athletes the chance to explore new techniques or strategies that interest them. This autonomy fosters a sense of control and personal investment in their sport, making it more enjoyable and fulfilling.

Ultimately, the goal is to create an environment where athletes feel supported, encouraged, and inspired to reach their potential without the weight of undue pressure. By focusing on progress using a process, setting achievable goals, celebrating every victory, and nurturing intrinsic motivation, you can help young athletes succeed in sports and develop a lifelong passion for learning and growth.

Emma coaches boys' hockey today and says, "Where do the kids' interests lie? Are they having fun? Where do they feel they can be themselves, on or off the ice?"

CREATING A POSITIVE TEAM CULTURE

Imagine a team stepping onto the field as individual players and a cohesive unit driven by shared values and goals. Establishing those core values is the first step in building a positive team culture. It's about collaboratively developing a mission statement that reflects what the team stands for and aims to achieve. This isn't just the coach's job; it's a collective effort where every player's voice is heard. Think of it as crafting the DNA of the team—a blend of respect, integrity, and teamwork. These values become the guiding principles that shape how the team interacts, competes, and grows together. Identifying these fundamental values sets the foundation for everything else, providing a common language and purpose that unites the team.

When a player comes to train, Eric lays out the structure to the parents, explaining what they do. He says, "We lay out our program for everybody and tell them how it works, and then it's up to them (if they want to participate). Unfortunately, it doesn't always work out. For some parents, that is a struggle. Everything has to be successful: every practice, every game, every swing, every throw. Everything has to be a win. Then we try to tell parents that we want the kids to fail now to learn."

Addressing conflicts head-on is also crucial. Open dialogue should be encouraged, allowing players to voice their concerns and resolve issues constructively. This approach resolves tensions and reinforces a culture of respect and understanding, where differences are seen as strengths rather than as obstacles.

Celebrating collaborative success is an integral part of developing a positive team culture. While individual accolades are essential, the focus should be on collective achievements. Recognizing team efforts during meetings or gatherings reinforces the idea that every player contributes to the team's success. It's about celebrating the group's victory with a team-first attitude.

Whether winning a championship or achieving a team goal, creating rituals or traditions to mark these successes can further strengthen team unity. Maybe it's a post-game tradition of sharing highlights or a team chant celebrating a win. These practices build a sense of belonging and pride, motivating players to continue striving for excellence as a team. By emphasizing collaborative success, players learn the value of teamwork and the importance of working together toward a common goal.

Modeling positive behavior is an essential responsibility for coaches and team leaders. They set the tone for the team, demonstrating the attitudes and behaviors they wish to see in their athletes. This means showing sportsmanship and fair play, both on and off the field. It's about leading by example, whether shaking hands with the opposing team or maintaining composure in challenging situations.

Positive communication and support among teammates are also crucial. Coaches and leaders should encourage players to uplift one another by offering encouragement and constructive feedback. This creates a supportive environment where players feel empowered to take risks and learn from their mistakes. By modeling these behaviors, coaches and leaders instill values beyond sports, shaping athletes into well-rounded individuals who carry these lessons into all areas of their lives.

Creating a positive team culture is an ongoing process. It requires commitment, collaboration, and a shared vision. As the team evolves, so will its culture, adapting to new challenges and opportunities. The foundation laid through core values, inclusivity, collaborative success, and positive modeling will guide the team through these changes, ensuring that it remains a supportive and empowering environment for all players. Whether on the field, in the locker room, or in everyday interactions, the impact of a positive team culture is profound, influencing the team's success and each athlete's growth and development.

UNDERSTANDING THE PARENT-COACH DYNAMIC

In the bustling world of youth sports, the parent-coach dynamic plays a pivotal role in shaping an athlete's experience. Parents and coaches each have distinct roles, and understanding these can make all the difference. Parents are the cheerleaders, the ones who provide emotional support and encouragement. They are there to offer a comforting word after a tough game or a high-five for a job well done. Coaches, on the other hand, are the strategists and mentors. They focus on developing skills, tactics, and teamwork.

The key to success is establishing clear boundaries between these roles. This means parents support their child's emotional needs without stepping into coaching territory, and coaches focus on athletic development without infringing on personal matters. Recognizing each party's unique contributions allows for a more harmonious relationship, ensuring the athlete benefits from both perspectives.

Eric Wood is the director of Player Development at Prospects Park in Englewood, CO. In his interview, he talks about how he teaches his players and works with the parents. "When I try to instruct, I ensure I don't tell them what they're doing wrong. What I try to do is make them do drills that force them to do what I want. We don't even need to talk. They have to execute the drill, which most of them can do; then they're doing the correct movement. Then, I don't have to put any doubt in their mind. As a coach, you see something; you know it's not correct. In your mind, the easiest thing to do is say, 'Hey, you're not doing that correctly.' Over time, that's not a good thing, as it can create doubt in the player's mind."

Creating a collaborative relationship between parents and coaches requires effort and understanding. One effective strategy is to schedule regular meetings to discuss the athlete's progress and any concerns.

These meetings provide a platform for open dialogue, where both parties can share insights and feedback. It's essential to approach these discussions with an open mind, valuing each other's input and expertise. Encouraging open communication helps build trust, ensuring everyone is on the same page regarding the athlete's development. This cooperation fosters a supportive environment where the athlete feels surrounded by a team dedicated to their growth. Parents and coaches can create a seamless support network that enhances the athlete's experience and performance by working together.

Disagreements are inevitable in any relationship, and the parent-coach dynamic is no exception. However, handling these conflicts constructively is crucial for maintaining a positive environment.

Focusing on the athlete's best interests during these discussions is essential, keeping their development and well-being at the forefront. From the outset, the parent needs to understand that it's up to the coach to bench a player and determine how much a player plays. This is where Eric has laid out how the system works when an athlete joins their team.

By addressing disagreements constructively, parents and coaches can prevent misunderstandings from escalating, ensuring that the focus remains on supporting the young athlete. This approach not only resolves conflicts but also strengthens the relationship between parents and coaches, leading to a more cohesive support system.

Empowering athletes to take ownership of their own development is a crucial aspect of their growth. Encouraging self-advocacy and decision-making helps athletes become more independent and confident in their abilities. By allowing athletes to take the lead in their own development, they become more invested in their journey, thus gaining valuable skills that extend beyond sports.

As we wrap up this chapter, it's clear that parent-coach collaboration is instrumental in nurturing young athletes. By clarifying roles, fostering communication, and supporting autonomy, we create an environment where athletes can thrive.

CHAPTER 11
THE FUTURE OF MENTAL TOUGHNESS TRAINING

" *In the future, mental strength will become the most critical aspect of any athlete's performance. Physical fitness can be trained, but mastering emotions and staying composed under pressure will be the ultimate edge.* "

NOVAK DJOKOVIC

The landscape of mental toughness training is shifting rapidly, driven by emerging trends and innovations. One of the most exciting developments is the integration of technology into mental training programs. Imagine stepping into a virtual reality environment designed to simulate high-pressure game scenarios.

Athletes can practice mental conditioning in a controlled setting that mimics real-life stressors, honing their focus and resilience without leaving the training facility. This technology provides a unique opportunity to prepare for the unpredictable nature of competitive sports, allowing athletes to experience and adapt to intense situations without the actual stakes. Advances in sports psychology and neuroscience are also playing a crucial role. Researchers are uncovering new insights into how the brain responds to stress and challenges, leading to more effective mental training techniques. Techniques that once seemed theoretical are now backed by science, offering athletes practical tools to enhance their mental game.

However, with these advancements come challenges and opportunities. As the pressure to succeed intensifies, athletes face increased stress and anxiety. Programs must adapt to support mental health, providing resources that help athletes manage these pressures while maintaining their performance. Additionally, training methods must evolve to meet the diverse needs of athletes. What works for one individual may not suit another, which calls for personalized approaches that consider each athlete's unique circumstances.

Experts in sports psychology and coaching are optimistic about the future. They predict that mental training techniques will continue to evolve, becoming more personalized and integrated into daily practice routines.

The next generation of athletes will likely approach mental toughness with the same rigor as physical training, recognizing its impact on overall performance. Coaches and psychologists emphasize the importance of creating a supportive environment that nurtures mental resilience from an early age, preparing athletes to handle the challenges of competition and the demands of life beyond sports.

Innovative practices are already shaping the future of mental toughness training. Personalized mental training apps offer customized exercises and feedback, allowing athletes to track their progress and adjust their strategies.

These tools make mental training more accessible, providing guidance anytime, anywhere. Virtual reality environments create immersive training experiences, challenging athletes to maintain focus and composure in simulated high-pressure situations. These innovations redefine how athletes approach mental training, making it an integral part of their development. As technology advances, possibilities for enhancing mental toughness become limitless, offering athletes new ways to train their minds alongside their bodies.

CONCLUSION

 "The vision of a champion is bent over, drenched in sweat, at the point of exhaustion, when nobody else is watching."

MIA HAMM - TWO-TIME FIFA WOMEN'S WORLD CUP CHAMPION

As we wrap up this journey together, let's take a moment to revisit the heart of what we've explored: the *Truth About Mental Toughness*. I hope you've learned that it's a vital part of the toolkit for all young athletes like you. The secret sauce, your "Razors' Edge," helps you bounce back from setbacks, power through challenges, and keep your eyes firmly on your goals. Whether on the court, field, or track, building resilience, confidence, and a growth mindset can set you up for success in sports and every aspect of your life.

Remember our deep dive into the traits that make mentally tough athletes stand out? We explored how grit, self-discipline, and courage are innate qualities and skills you can cultivate with dedication and practice. As I said at the start, you're in charge of your journey and have the power to be your own superhero in sports and beyond.

We delved into self-reflection and goal achieving, visualization, journaling, self-talk, and more, offering you tools to understand your strengths and identify areas for improvement. This isn't about perfection but creating a process for progress. Small incremental changes over time manifest into massive changes down the road. By knowing yourself better, you become better equipped to tackle challenges head-on.

As we discussed, failure isn't the end of the road—it's a stepping stone. By viewing setbacks as opportunities for growth, you can transform obstacles into powerful motivators. Remember those inspiring stories and quotes from Emma, Michael, Eric, and Jasper, all professional athletes who turned their failures into fuel for success. Let them remind you that resilience can lead you to the heights you are after.

Drawing from these lessons, the takeaway is clear: Mental toughness is a journey, not a destination. It's about embracing the process and understanding that every challenge you face is an opportunity to grow stronger. Whether you're overcoming pre-game jitters or managing expectations, the skills you've learned in this book will serve as a foundation for your continued growth.

Now, it's time for action. Take these insights and strategies and weave them into your daily life. Use this book as a reference to build your process to excel. Practice the exercises, embrace the mindset shifts, and don't shy away from the challenging moments. These are the building blocks of your mental toughness. Share your journey with teammates, coaches, and family. Together, you can create a supportive network that uplifts and inspires.

But remember, this book is just the beginning. Your journey doesn't end here; it continues with every step you take. Keep pushing your boundaries, setting new goals, and striving for excellence. The world of sports and beyond is full of opportunities waiting for you to seize them.

As you look to the future, envision a path where your mental toughness guides you, not only in your athletic pursuits but in all facets of life. See yourself tackling challenges confidently, leading with empathy, and inspiring others with resilience. This vision isn't just a dream; it's within your reach. You can achieve greatness and leave a lasting impact with the right mindset and dedication.

Thank you for allowing me to be a part of your journey. I'm passionate about helping you become the best version of yourself. I hope this book has given you the tools and inspiration to do just that. Here's to your continued success and the exciting adventures that lie ahead. Remember, you have the power to be unbreakable. Keep believing in yourself and never stop growing.

========================

You'll find the links to the Pro Interviews after the next page.

MAKE A DIFFERENCE WITH YOUR REVIEW

Thank you for joining me on this incredible journey through the world of Mental Toughness in Sports and for Young Athletes. I hope that you found your exploration as enlightening and inspiring as I did when writing this book for you. As we close this chapter together, I have a small favor to ask—**a moment of your time for a big impact!**

Could you please leave a review? Sharing your thoughts on Amazon helps guide others who are curious about the exciting possibilities of Mental Toughness.

Your review will empower others to navigate the ups and downs of becoming the best they can be as an athlete and person. Your review makes it easier for them to discover this book and embark on their own journey in the world of sports excellence.

Leaving a review is quick, but the impact is lasting. Whether it's a detailed account of how you applied the insights from the book or a quick note on which chapter you loved the most, your thoughts are incredibly valuable and greatly appreciated.

Scan the QR code to leave a review:

Thank you once again for your time and support. Here's to your future in the exhilarating world of sports and beyond—may it be as limitless as your potential to achieve and transform yourself. Keep building and improving your process for training and in life. Most importantly, keep sharing your journey!

- Tony Neumeyer

BONUS INTERVIEWS STRAIGHT FROM THE PROS

As promised, here are the links to the four interviews done specifically for this book. I want to thank each of these professionals for taking their time and allowing me to use their words and thoughts as part of this project and book. I truly believe their insights are invaluable and set this book apart from others. I encourage you to watch each of the discussions in its entirety, they are all very different and I believe you can insights that could prove priceless.

Micheal Saunders Interview Link: https://
bit.ly/SaundersToughness (35:48)

Michael Saunders is a former professional baseball outfielder, drafted by the Seattle Mariners in 2004. Known for his strong arm and power at the plate, Saunders played eight seasons in Major League Baseball, spending most of his career with the Mariners, followed by stints with the  Toronto Blue Jays and the Philadelphia Phillies. He briefly played for the Colorado Rockies during his later years. After retiring from professional baseball, Saunders transitioned into coaching and player development, sharing his expertise with young athletes while also working on community-based initiatives to promote sports and wellness.

Emma Vlasic Interview Link: https://bit.ly/EmmaToughness
(34:44)

Emma Vlasic is a talented professional hockey player who has made a name for herself in women's hockey. Known for her strong leadership and skill as a forward, she played collegiate hockey at Yale University before moving on to play professionally in the National Women's Hockey League (NWHL), now known as the Premier Hockey Federation (PHF). Emma's hockey IQ, work ethic, and offensive prowess have made her a standout player. Today, she continues to inspire young athletes by promoting women's hockey and staying active in youth development programs, where she mentors the next generation of female hockey players. Today she continues her career at Hedgeye Research, an independent financial research firm that provides individuals to fund managers daily macro market inputs to consistently beat the market.

Eric Wood Interview Link: https://bit.ly/WoodToughness
(43:06)

Eric Wood is a former professional baseball player who spent time in the Pittsburgh Pirates organization. As a versatile infielder and outfielder, he demonstrated solid defensive skills and was known for his consistent bat in the minor leagues. Wood played primarily at third base but showed flexibility across the diamond, earning him a reputation as a dependable utility player. After his baseball career, Eric has shifted focus to coaching, working with young athletes to develop their skills and mental toughness, while also staying involved in community initiatives.

Jasper Blake Interview Link: https://bit.ly/BlakeToughness
(1:01:52)

Jasper Blake is a Canadian professional triathlete, coach, and endurance sports expert known for his achievements in Ironman and long-distance racing. Born and raised in Canada, Blake became one of the country's top triathletes, winning **Ironman Canada in 2006** and earning  multiple podium finishes throughout his career. Renowned for his mental toughness and strategic racing approach, he transitioned into coaching, helping aspiring triathletes and endurance athletes reach their peak performance. With a strong focus on mindset, resilience, and training efficiency, Blake continues to inspire the next generation of athletes through coaching, public speaking, and mentorship.

REFERENCES

Mental Toughness in Sport: Athletes Judged to Be Mentally Tough Perform Better. https://psychology.org.au/for-members/publications/inpsych/2018/december-issue-6/analyse-this/mental-toughness-in-sport

Revisiting Growth Mindset as a Core Capacity of Sport Psychology. https://applied sportpsych.org/blog/2021/04/revisiting-growth-mindset-as-a-core-capacity-of-sport-psychology

17 Famous Examples of Mental Toughness. https://drrobbell.com/17-famous-exam ples-of-mental-toughness

The Sporting Resilience Model: A Systematic Review of Resilience in Sports Performers. https://pmc.ncbi.nlm.nih.gov/articles/PMC9811683

Grit and Athletic Performance. https://www.trine.edu/academics/centers/center-for-sports-studies/blog/2021/grit_and_athletic_performance.aspx

How to Build Self-Discipline as an Athlete. https://www.successstartswithin.com/sports-psychology-articles/athlete-mental-toughness/how-to-build-self-disci pline-as-an-athlete

10 Inspiring Athletes: Stories of Perseverance and Success in the World of Sports. https://kowloonsports.com/gb/itblog/18_Inspiring-Athletes.html

Courage Under Pressure: What 5 Iconic Sports Moments Can Teach Us About Conquering Fear. https://blog.bsnsports.com/articles/courage-under-pressure-what-5-iconic-sports-moments-can-teach-us-about-conquering-fear

The Importance of Self-Reflection in Sports Performance Environments. https://www.linkedin.com/pulse/importance-self-reflection-sports-performance-joseph-janner

The Ultimate Guide to SMART Goals for Student-Athletes. https://productivere cruit.com/blog/smart-goals-for-student-athletes

Resilience: The Ways to Enhance This Critical Skill in Sports. https://broadviewpsy chology.com/2020/04/21/resilience-the-ways-to-enhance-this-critical-skill-in-sports

Self-Awareness in Athletes. https://optimizemindperformance.com/self-awareness-in-athletes

Olympians Use Imagery as Mental Training. https://www.nytimes.com/2014/02/23/sports/olympics/olympians-use-imagery-as-mental-training.html

The Power of a Positive Mental Attitude in Sports: How It Affects Performance.

https://www.benjaminbonetti.com/blogs/articles-reviews/the-power-of-a-positive-mental-attitude-in-sports-how-it-affects-performance

4 Types of Self-Talk Involved in Sports Performance. https://optimumjoy.com/blog/4-types-of-self-talk-involved-in-sports-performance-zach-seifert

Why You Need to Be Process Focused as an Athlete. https://www.successstartswithin.com/sports-psychology-articles/focus-training-for-sports/why-you-need-to-be-processed-focused-as-an-athlete

Mindfulness Training Enhances Endurance Performance and Executive Functions in Athletes: An Event-Related Potential Study. https://www.ncbi.nlm.nih.gov/pmc/articles/PMC7474752

How Sports Psychologists Help Athletes Handle Pressure. https://www.performanceperspectives.com.au/sport-psychology/how-sports-psychologists-help-athletes-handle-pressure

Mental Rehearsal Might Prepare Our Minds for Action. https://news.stanford.edu/stories/2018/02/mental-rehearsal-might-prepare-minds-action

Michael Jordan's Handling of Failure Was a Powerful Part of His Success. https://drstankovich.com/michael-jordans-handling-of-failure-was-a-powerful-part-of-his-success

Developing Mental Strength and Resilience in Youth Athletes. https://www.jamesleath.com/notes/developing-mental-strength-and-resilience-in-youth-athletes

10 Incredible Sports Comebacks That Fans Will Never Forget. https://www.menshealth.com/entertainment/g60970446/best-sports-comebacks

Learning From Mistakes: Handling Criticism Like a Pro Athlete. https://www.athletesmentaltrainer.com/blog/2024/09/26/learning-from-mistakes-handling-criticism-like-a-pro-athlete

7 Strategies for Overcoming Sports Performance Anxiety https://www.performancepsychologycenter.com/post/sports-performance-anxiety

Breathing Techniques and Benefits for Athletes by Subash Mathi. https://www.athleticlab.com/breathing-techniques-and-benefits-for-athletes-by-subash-mathi

Courage Under Pressure: What 5 Iconic Sports Moments Can Teach Us About Conquering Fear. https://blog.bsnsports.com/articles/courage-under-pressure-what-5-iconic-sports-moments-can-teach-us-about-conquering-fear

The Effects of Nutritional Interventions on the Cognitive Development of Preschool-Age Children: A Systematic Review. https://www.ncbi.nlm.nih.gov/pmc/articles/PMC8839299

Sleep Better, Play Better: 5 Tips to Optimize Sleep for Youth Athletes. https://www.teamelitechiropractic.com/post/sleep-better-play-better-5-tips-to-optimize-sleep-for-youth-athletes

Mastering Time Management for Student Athletes. https://www.athleteplus.org/mastering-time-management-for-student-athletes

Creating Positive Sports Environments and Intervention Strategies to Handle Challenges. https://positivecoach.org/resource-zone/creating-positive-sports-environments-and-intervention-strategies-to-handle-challenges

Boosting Mental Toughness in Young Athletes & 20 Strategies. https://positivepsychology.com/mental-toughness-for-young-athletes

The Game-Changing Power of Journaling in Sport Psychology. https://rjperformance.medium.com/the-game-changing-power-of-journaling-in-sport-psychology-4500ff7400d7

Mental Training Exercises for Sports. https://www.successstartswithin.com/sports-psychology-articles/athlete-mental-training/mental-training-exercises-for-sports

Building a Culture of Mental Toughness: The Pyramid Model. https://www.championshipproductions.com/cgi-bin/champ/p/Performance-Training/The-Athletes-Playbook-Building-a-Culture-of-Mental-Toughness-The-Pyramid-Model_GB-00978.html

The 4 Cs of Effective Communication for Coaches. https://completeperformancecoaching.com/2021/08/21/the-4-cs-of-effective-communication-for-coaches

To Push or Not to Push: Finding the Balance in Kids Sports. https://the-cauldron.com/to-push-or-not-to-push-finding-the-balance-in-kids-sports-38a67ffcda84

Create the Right Sports Team Culture: 10 Critical Factors. https://www.athleteassessments.com/ten-critical-aspects-to-create-the-right-sports-team-culture

Teamwork: How to Make the Most of The Coach-Parent Dynamic. https://truesport.org/teamwork/make-most-of-coach-parent-dynamic

From Rags to Riches: Inspiring Stories of Athletes Overcoming Adversity. https://medium.com/@informationexplained73/from-rags-to-riches-inspiring-stories-of-athletes-overcoming-adversity-26a1c3b229ef

Life After Sport: Why Athletes Need to Prepare. https://olympics.com/athlete365/articles/a365-topic-career-plus/life-after-sport-why-athletes-need-to-prepare

Mental Toughness: The Key to Athletic Success. https://www.trine.edu/academics/centers/center-for-sports-studies/blog/2021/mental_toughness_the_key_to_athletic_success.aspx